Praise

"Through the lens of fatherhood, Dan Szczesny demonstrates what it means to be mindful, curious, and awakened. Readers travel through time, experiencing the first five years of Uma's life through her father's eyes. Dan takes his vast knowledge and condenses it in a way that brings readers into the moment and goes directly to the heart. He beautifully captures how the moments that create our memories and build relationships are opportunities for connection and enlightenment. Dan and Uma show us that all we are seeking is right here, in every moment. We just need the eyes to see it."

—Kourtney LaFavre, author of If Sun Could Speak
and mom of four kids

"In today's world where life moves far too quickly, what a delight to stumble upon this beautiful collection. Like a time capsule full of wondrous observations, we are all at once transported to a slower, more thoughtful world where we witness the passage of time through the eyes of a loving dad. Dan Szczesny's delight and simultaneous grief over the inevitable growth of his precious and oh-so-wise young daughter will resonate with me for a long time to come."

—Kasey Mathews, speaker, coach and author of Preemie:
Lessons in Love, Life and Motherhood *and* A Mom's
Guide to Creating a Magical Life, *and mom of two kids*

"Lovely and lively reflections on the world of being a dad. One of the purest joys of parenting is that you get to be there as your child becomes who they are, and, as it happens, you often find out a lot about who *you* are too. These essays show that even as parenting (along with everything else) gets more and more complex,

Dan Szczesny keeps this simple, straightforward and important truth close by. If anyone is meant to be a dad and then to write about how special that can be, then he certainly is."

—*Brady Carlson, author of* Dead Presidents: An American Adventure into the Strange Deaths *and* Surprising Afterlives of Our Nation's Leaders, *and dad of three kids*

"Dan Szczesny's connection to our world flows off the page and into us, harkening back to the earthen intuition of the native New England transcendentalists of old, but infused with the complex wisdom and lightness of heart of one who's watched the twentieth century blend clumsily into the twenty-first. Where the book shines, however, is in his palpable connection with his daughter and grasp of the gifts both of childhood and, especially, of parenthood. Within each short, meditative chapter, we not only see life through Dan's insightful eyes—which miss nothing about this enchanted, ordinary place—but we see the kind of parent that we ourselves aspire to be."

—*Chris DiLoreto, Creative Director,* Monadnock Underground, *and dad of three kids*

During my very first nannying gig, I was sternly attempting to coerce my young charge to walk down the sidewalk on a beautiful afternoon. He ignored me, squatting down and squealing, "It's a sign of spring!" at a tiny violet unfurling from a crack in the sidewalk. In this book, Dan Szczesny offers us a dazzling handful of these gems, illuminating a deeply spiritual dimension of parenthood. His stories about experiences with his daughter invite us to open ourselves to the hints of the divine that grow in unexpected cracks, even when they arrive crying at 2:00 AM or dressed in a superhero cape.

—*Zoë Wroten-Heinzmann, Religious Educator at the Unitarian Universalist Church of Peterborough, and mom of two kids*

You & Me

reflections on becoming your dad

Dan Szczesny

The Hobblebush Reflections Series, Volume I

HOBBLEBUSH BOOKS
Concord, New Hampshire

The essay "Here There Be Dragons" was previously published in the *Monadnock Underground*. Several of these essays appeared in different forms in the *Good Men Project* and the *Monadnock Underground*.

Composed in Adobe Caslon Pro at Hobblebush Books

Printed in the United States of America

ISBN: 978-1-939449-22-1

Library of Congress Control Number: 2020938692

The Hobblebush Reflections Series, Volume I
Edited by Kirsty Walker

HOBBLEBUSH BOOKS
PO Box 1285
Concord, NH 03302

www.hobblebush.com

To Uma and Meenakshi

CONTENTS

PREFACE

I never set out to write a book about my daughter. And many would say this book is about me, not her.

My intention, originally, was to keep a journal for her. It would be a way that someday, she'd be able to look back on her life through my eyes. I wanted to just write her history for her.

But life has a way of changing your plans.

On the day she was born, my wife, Meena, had a postpartum hemorrhage. In about twenty minutes, we went from momma time with our newborn to emergency surgery. There was a whole world of unknowns exploding in my head as I sat in the nursery, trying to engage with my baby daughter, the nurses there desperate to take my mind off the terrible blow fate appeared to be handing us.

In the weeks and months of uncertainty and recovery that followed, I began to turn to that journal as a way of both recording the events unfolding for my daughter and also as a way to help me deal and, indeed, to try to heal. As it sometimes does, my writing became therapeutic.

I'd post photos and snippets on social media as parents do and would engage with our friends and family that came together to help in those early days. And we began to realize we weren't alone—that birth wasn't as easy and romantic as it was often portrayed. That we, in many ways, got lucky. We were still together, fighting, getting better, day after—sometimes painful—day.

Through the words, I began to see a group of parents and guardians and family forming that had the same questions about life, the same sense of something bigger than themselves filtered through the everyday work of diapers and teething, filtered through the pain of scraped knees and broken bones.

Writing about the wonders and agony of parenting became a way for me to channel my own creativity toward questions I've long held about philosophy, spirituality, and our role in our own lives and in the lives of others. Parenting became a sort of religion, and I became an eager student.

I wrote directly to my daughter like an epistolary novel to her about her life. Someday, maybe, she'll be able to hear my voice through these letters.

As time went on, the passages became longer and more complex. As she grew and changed and learned, so did I. The questions became deeper, the answers less certain.

And a critical understanding of my role in her life—and by association, my life—began to emerge: that I had to become content with not knowing things and with finding joy and awe in the glorious mess of parenting where the next day, sometimes the next minute, offers yet another unknown; there is rarely a road map.

I came to look forward to these bouts of not knowing, excited about the next thing to learn, the next tidal wave of organic information. Accepting that the next day would bring yet another challenge that I couldn't possibly predict became calming, in fact—like the purest form of living mindfully.

This was the ultimate way of living life in the moment.

I hope this small, chronological collection of essays—addressed to her but written for me—also offers the reader some moments of pause. I've used the five Chinese elements of wuxing (earth, fire, wood, water, and metal) as a way to structure each of my daughter's first five years and as a means of pulling the essays out into their purest, open form.

Kids or not, may you all spin through your days in the moment, may you all have many questions, and may you all lead an interesting life. Onward!

Dan Szczesny
Manchester, New Hampshire
March 2020

year one
EARTH

REBIRTH

As midnight approaches on the last day of 2014, I am finally able to breathe—deep, long inhales weighted with insomnia and boiled in fear and uncertainty. But breathing is a start.

From the corner of our maternity room, I'm able to look out over the city toward the river. The room is dark, the hospital quiet. You mother breathes on her own now, the tubes gone, fewer wires and electrodes. In between her bed and the chair where I sit is the rolling, transparent bassinet where you sleep on your back in a swaddle of my own design. I promise I'll get better at the swaddle, baby.

Twenty-four hours ago, none of this was certain.

From the corner of my eye, a red and white flash appears out my window in the distance. The new year is nearly here. I am awake alone, and somewhere across town a splash of fireworks begins the countdown to your first full year. We are fortunate that the year will begin with your mother at our side.

I am unable to sleep, of course; it's been nearly three days now since your mother went into labor—through the terrible delivery and uncertain hours—and now we're finally here. I feel the ache of exhaustion in my bones, but to shut my eyes now—to not hear the breathing of you and of your mother—feels like an abandonment, like if I stay awake, if I remain vigilant, that alone will protect you both.

I have no idea now, only forty-eight hours into your life, how different my sleep patterns will remain for years. Forever maybe. For now, as the fireworks cast a colorful glow on your tiny face, I bend my ear to your lips and feel your breath on my cheek.

In my mind swirls thoughts of rebirth, new chances. Expectant parents are so often told that once the baby is born, their old lives die.

But as I consider the past year, it also occurs to me that nothing but the past day matters anyway. On the last day of 2014, I fed you for the first time. I changed your diaper for the first time. Your mommy ate solid food for the first time since delivery. I listened to her snore, not for the first time, but the sound this time was beautiful. My dinner was homemade curry, cooked and packed and brought to me by your grandma. I talked to my sister, your aunt. I hugged our other "adopted" children, Aaron and Janelle. I wrote these words.

Perhaps my old life is gone, baby. But what they don't tell you is that it's replaced by something more amazing. Of all the wondrous things I have seen and done in my blessed life, on the last day of 2014, I did nothing, and it was everything.

* * *

A few days on and your mother has begun to take her first few steps on her own. We have all sunk into a routine here in the hospital's maternity ward. I found Popsicles in the hall fridge, and we've begun seeing an influx of family and friends, all eager to see you, baby, but equally relieved to see your mother.

With plans to leave soon, it occurs to us that the hospital has a tradition. As a newly minted mom is moving from labor to maternity after giving birth, she gets to push a special button on the wall. It plays a chime that rings through the hospital, signifying a new baby has been born. In the scare that followed your birth, your mother never pushed that button. You never chimed into the world.

So today your mother gets up out of bed, and taking slow, deliberate steps, walks on her own power out of the maternity ward, through the long hall, and into the labor ward where the team of nurses and doctors who delivered you waits.

We often think of medical professionals as distant or cold, but there are many moist eyes there as they watch your mother take the final steps to that chime. Then, one more remarkable moment as she insists that I push that button with her.

So, six days after you entered the world, standing in a cold hallway surrounded by people who for a moment are not nurses and doctors but just human beings, your parents pushed that damn button.

And in that moment, this small symbolic afterthought becomes our life reboot. That silly nursery melody becomes a symphony that signals both our arrival as a family and our rebirth.

Through the years, I have paid witness to your mother's

discipline and determination. But, baby, nothing has come close to watching her push a tiny red button in a long bare hallway on a snowy winter evening in Manchester, New Hampshire. Nothing.

* * *

The days roll by like current in a stream. We move to a routine that is slowly becoming familiar.

Sleep. Pee. Change. Eat. Burp. Poop. Change. Play.

Repeat, sometimes quickly, sometimes with great space between. Today, with your grandma, we dress you in a brand-new outfit, a tiny red tunic, while you squiggle and giggle and yell. I understand that your smiles are only biology at this stage, your little brain synapses firing up neurons and taking those cheek muscles for trial runs. But still, that smile . . .

I won't know this for sure until many years have passed, little girl, but I'm inclined to believe that this may be the best time of my life.

THE BEAR BEHIND US

Better. Slowly.

After the difficult last couple weeks, we slowly ease into the routine of our new life.

We are careful now, and when someone asks us how we are, we simply say, "better." Baby, you envelop our thoughts and days and time, and you continue to be a touchstone for our whole family, a tiny brilliant light of hope and energy and love. For a sentimentalist like myself, it's important to gain insight from a more pragmatic thinker. I often turn to one of my favorite filmmakers, Werner Herzog, to keep me grounded in times of emotional crisis.

Once, when asked if he had any advice about dealing with life, he said, "Get used to the bear behind you." Just days ago, it seems like all we did was look over our shoulders. But now, baby, with you protecting us, we find ourselves in the moment more often, getting "better" at dealing with that bear.

One month ago, it felt as though we might lose everything. After the anticipation, excitement, and all the plans, you had far different ideas about your arrival. Or perhaps it wasn't you at all.

Maybe it was simply chaos without order or care. Maybe there was unpaid karmic debt. Maybe it was a test to determine the strength of our character.

Maybe life just flings dung at you and laughs.

But yesterday, with your mother on her feet and stepping strongly day by day into being a mom, we gathered with our little misfit family and lit the candle on a one-month birthday cupcake.

And each of us—your grandparents, your dear friends— took turns holding you, passing you around like a battery to draw life and energy from. I felt like lifting you above my head toward the heavens.

See? I would shout through my anger. *We're still standing!*

But instead, I delicately cut the cupcake, and you gurgle and squirm, and each of us, someplace deep inside, silently begins to bury the fear. And slowly, cautiously, unwilling to disturb whatever truce we may have brokered with the universe, we begin to feel relief. And hope.

Slowly. Better.

GO EASY

If I lay my hand on your chest, I can feel your heartbeat vibrating through my fingertips. You still seem so impossibly fragile. The days and hours find a rhythm. Sometimes the moments, too. The mornings come fast amid occasional jags of uncertainty of what to do. I go down my check list. You're still crying. What now?

But today, a new moment to consider. Maybe you don't need anything. Maybe you just want to give. So, on the first day of your fifth week in our world, and on the day before my own birthday, a gift. I tickle your feet and you smile, and this time it seems like a real smile, deliberate. I am smitten.

I know your reactions are not specific; you're tired, you're little, you just want to feel warm and safe. But can there be anything more primal than sitting with you in a rocking chair as you burrow deep into the crook of my arm?

I just fed you. I pull you closer. I whisper in your ear.

And you trust me. After only a few weeks you decide that I won't hurt you, that I can give you warmth and a full belly and quiet when you need it. In your sleep, you murmur. And it's like the entirety of time itself comes crashing into my heart, all because of a rocker that used to belong to my father and a content baby and everything that is now.

When these moments happen, I work to hold them because

not all nights have sleep. Not all nights are calm. Some nights, you are so restless, you're unable to express anything but rage and tears. But even those nights end sometime, and when you finally decide to have pity on me and I'm able to throw myself onto the futon for a fragile hour-long nap, fitful and light, I wake to the sound of giggles and squeals and stumble into the bedroom to discover you and your momma taking selfies.

You see me and shriek in one long, high-pitched wail, your version of a laugh—and the two of you grin and my sleepless night is forgotten.

So go easy on me, baby. Soon, your mom will head back to work, and with daycare still a few months away, that means we'll be taking a run at this thing called life together—the two of us—just like we started from the beginning. Then, I rocked with you in the nursery without any idea what I was doing—entirely unable to know what any of your sounds, your moves, your looks, meant. I guessed at everything, often got it wrong, kept one eye on your mother as she recovered. But even then, when you were only hours old and the ground under my feet seemed ready to collapse at any moment, you would bury your tiny nose into the crook of my arm and your little hands would quiver and you'd make a noise like a wispy sigh, like you were letting go of fear. And you got me through. You gave me faith and energy. That little gesture, a shudder where your shoulders would drop and your fists unclench, was like a transfer of power. I got that.

Now, at 3:00 AM after a particularly hard day full of temper and rage and exasperation, you are finally quiet. And just as

I'm once again at the edge of the abyss, you turn your little head toward me and bury your nose in my arm, take a long, deep breath and close your eyes, and I get it, I feel it. So go easy on me, baby, I understand so much more now.

Let me give back. Let's do this together. I've been thinking a lot, baby, about time and the days gone by. Weird, right? We still have a long way to go, and yet the weeks rush by so fast I sometimes feel like I'm caught in deep current, just hanging on, staying afloat, helpless. At first, of course, there was fear and injury, and every single night—sometimes every single hour—felt like a victory, a small step away from the darkness. But then it changed.

Your mother got stronger. And you grew out of your newborn clothes, and suddenly our focus shifted from medication and hospital visits to diaper size and types of formula, and just like that we were parents having the same conversations as all the rest, and it felt so suddenly real. And then you smiled. And then you had nights where you would not sleep. And then you had gas. And then . . . then you laughed when I walked into a room and you recognized my voice and looked up at me and I thought, my God, we're doing this, you are my daughter.

Now we have a bag of clothes that no longer fit you, and I feel like I'm staring down at the beginning of an amazing meal, but feeling sad because I know that plate will soon be empty. So I refocus on the high points that are now—your smile, your eyelashes, how you kick with all of your might and pedal the air and lift up your little head and scream with joy at the sun. And maybe the epiphany here is that those moments will never end. They may change, but they will keep coming, one after another after another. And my job is to simply be aware of them.

My job is to bathe in the ever-changing light.

ONE HUNDRED DAYS

There is a moment when the three of us are all together, with the sun streaming into the nursery and the house quiet, when you just stop and look up and wait. And we stop, too, and just watch you. You smile. You are calm. You're okay with us and we, you. Tomorrow, after nearly one hundred days, your mother returns to work. Despite the challenges of those first few weeks, being with each other every day—through every meal and every late-night cry, every doctor visit and every pot of tea or warmed cup of milk—seems impossible. What family has that chance? One hundred days. A lifetime and a blink of an eye. My heart aches in anticipation of this new chapter.

And there's something else. How fitting for this first, amazing few months in your life to come to a close on Easter Day. After all, it was exactly one year ago today that I discovered I was to be your dad. Over the course of one year, bookended by a day designed to celebrate fertility and new life, I have watched you grow, baby, and then watched your mother struggle against the darkness and emerge bolder and stronger. We left the hospital with new friends to help us face down the fear, then watched our family surround us with love and life and tenderness in ways that saved our lives.

I've watched my nephews argue over who was to hold their new baby cousin, and just now, before sitting down to write my thoughts, I've watched you fall asleep in my arms. It's all too much, too easy to say we are blessed or fortunate. I am no fool, baby, and I understand the universe does not cater exclusively to us. The universe owes me nothing.

But today, as we three sat on the bed in silence, holding hands, just watching and doing nothing except being together, for just one moment, the universe is ours.

* * *

Weeks later, in scope and degree, our days float in and out of a sleepy haze of tiny milestones. You stretch out to grasp a bottle. You grab your pacifier, take it out of your mouth, and hold it in your hand for ten seconds. You half-turn, hilariously get stuck in mid-roll, and have a fit about it. In between naps, I rush to live—laundry, dishes, cooking; I try to get some words down on paper. But I don't actually want to do any of that. I'd rather just nap when you do, then watch in amazement as you watch me. This is hard work—being a dad at home to a baby, the hardest thing I'm ever likely to do and easy compared to what's yet to come. But I often feel so certain that at any moment you could lift up off your crib and fly, and how sad would that be for me to miss such a miracle?

Systems. Schedules. Routines. Days roll by in a comfortable series of old habits and new explorations. I never thought I'd look forward to moments that during my past life would have seemed mundane, so uninvolved. Now I watch the clock, thinking ahead to what new outfit we'll try today, or when your mom will come home so we can take a walk through the neighborhood. I once gazed at Everest. Now I look on with the same sense of wonder and awe as you grab my glasses for the first time and fling them across the room and laugh at me. And I laugh too, because why wouldn't I? Look at you!

Others know this. Many, many before me have been down the same trail. I'm not breaking new ground here, I know. But to me it may as well be a new planet, breathing different air, seeing a different landscape around every turn, no context except to realize that every day is something new. And to roll on and on, into the horizon.

THE RAIN

This morning, I wake to a heaviness of heart—one of those days that I can feel in my bones—hard and long and uncertain. Outside, the rain roars and the house is cold, and as I wish your mother goodbye and remind her to drive safe, I want nothing else but for her to stay home, to drink tea with me, to talk about things I miss, like hiking big mountains and running off to the movies and walking through the streets of Boston or New York without care.

And when you wake up, just moments after your mother leaves, not giving me enough time to even make coffee, I feel a rare frustration. Here's another day of diapers and peek-a-boo and the world goes by outside and I am no longer part of that. In a sort of dreary haze, I wander out onto the porch with you in my arms, not remembering the cold and the rain. And as we step outside, a wave of chilly rain, carried by the wind, splashes us both.

My reaction? Anger and dejection. But not you. You laugh. You roar and laugh at the rain and the waterfall coming down off our roof into the gutters and the birds screeching in puddles. You put your wet hands to your mouth and touch your drippy cheeks and your whole body shakes in joy, legs kicking, arms pinwheeling.

Six months in and you are still my strength when my heart

is drained. Six months ago, I could not possibly have imagined the depth and weight of this journey. I still can't, I guess. But I'm still surprised. Every day. By my family. By your mother's amazing fortitude. By your eyes and hair and cheeks. By the rain I've seen a million times, but never through your eyes.

This is all so fragile and impermanent yet cast in the forge of millions of stars over millions of years. In your eyes, I see the reflection of my own dreams and family and everyone whose path we have crossed and everyone who will touch our lives to come. And I am overwhelmed by it all, this connection, this direct line unbroken. A path that began at the beginning of everything and a tether that will remain in the very atoms of the clouds long, long, long after our journey together comes to a close. I am not qualified to define us; I'm too small and it is all so big. But I know that we are only and incredibly stardust, and that today, the rain will do. In fact, the rain is wonderful.

EARTH

This morning, we take our final walk of your first summer. As usual, I work hard to be in the present with you, to relish these fleeting mornings. Each walk is like a live jazz solo, always different, never a duplicate, and most importantly, never coming back—singular in its uniqueness in time and place and of the bond that we create every day we're together.

Today though, we both feel change in the air and in the dirt under our feet—literally, as a sharp breeze drops down into your stroller and you turn your head away and frown, and figuratively, as I understand that this particular solo, this chapter, this glorious song, is nearly at an end. Now, it seems like every day—every hour—is a complex dance of opening and closing, of lasts and firsts. For every pang of sadness when you no longer fit into a favorite jumper or will no longer sleep in the rocker or decide, finally, that peas are no longer part of your diet, there is a first. The first tooth, the first kiss, the first time you stand on your own and clap. Every moment is a new moment, every moment is the end and the beginning. And here we are, the end of summer, the end of rebirth, the beginning of red leaves and pumpkins. We take our time today out there, listening to the melody of our urban music wind down.

For once, baby, you're mellow, not fussing at all. Perhaps, like me, you feel the changes, the beginnings, the endings.

You look up at me from the stroller carriage, your cheeks pink and your eyes shimmer in the cool sun. As I've been doing the past few walks, I stroll through a nearby garden cemetery. Fall has begun to reveal itself early this year, and the tree-thick burial ground with its smooth paths and leaf-popping color is a favorite and calming route for us.

The day is mellow, so I walk casually through the winding paths. We're alone here. I notice a curious section of the cemetery, and we go to explore. But once I realize what it is, I wish I hadn't come.

This small area, tucked off into a hidden corner, is an area for children burials. The stones are small and close to the ground. There are trinkets everywhere, beads and stickers. One tiny marker reads just the name *Benjamin*. Buried a few inches into the earth at Benjamin's stone is a small plastic fire truck, the elements stripping the toy down to a light pink faded color.

Suddenly, it's all too much for me—this past year, the close calls when you were born, the hours and daily work. I can feel panic creeping into my shoulders.

But you sigh loudly, pulling me back into focus, and the moment passes. I push us out of there, too quickly perhaps. But I want us to be home now. I want to escape to our favorite rocker, to be away from the permanence of the clay.

And slowly, the song returns—the leaves and the birds and the wind. In time, you close your eyes and drift off, signaling our last bow to summer. The next time we ride, we'll welcome crisp fall, and the music—different, more complex—will play again.

MY ONLY SUNSHINE

Dear baby,

You're up, again, at 5:00 AM, needy. I lift you out of your crib and pace the cold floor in the dark, and you look up at me, quiet, awake, teary-eyed. Like you're waiting for something. And then I remember. Today is your first birthday, and now, almost to the minute, is the time when you came, the time of thunder and chaos. The time when we had everything, and almost lost it all.

And the thought of those days, now exactly one year ago, makes my legs go weak. I sit in the rocking chair. Left with no other spell to ward off the darkness, I sing, just as I did to you in the hospital nursery when you were only an hour old.

You are my sunshine . . .

I sing this because back then, I knew no other song, knew of no other protection for you, for your mother, as we waited to hear our fate, alone, you swaddled in my arms, your heat and breath on my cheek.

My only sunshine . . .

And even now, one year later, those moments are so vivid I can feel the hard slats of that hospital rocking chair against my back, the squeak of it on the linoleum, the blinding lights and wide windows and the nurses' concerned looks, trying to distract me, to keep me calm.

You make me happy when skies are grey . . .

And how even then, only minutes old, I could feel how strong you were, how strong you'd be. I drew on that strength; seven pounds of soft flesh that in those solitary, confusing few moments was the only thing that grounded me to sanity. Was I singing to you? Was I singing to your mother? Was I praying?

You'll never know dear, how much I love you . . .

Now, as then, your eyes flutter and you sigh, like you know what day it is. Are you protecting me again?

Please don't take my sunshine away.

But unlike then, we are here, the three of us. One year on. And as the darkness turns to day, I keep you tight against my chest as you fall asleep and I listen, grateful, to the stirs of your mother who is safe. One year on, baby. I don't know if you know, but I think you do, that you are our sun and moon and stars.

Happy Birthday, darling, and thank you. May you always burn like the sun and explode like thunder!

Your dad

year two
FIRE

EVERY WAKING MOMENT

The day is warm, though still winter, and I swear I can smell summer in the air. But you are having none of that.

You're fussy and miserable—nearly unhinged and high energy—from the moment you open your eyes, wanting your way and only your way, but I have no idea what that way is.

So we get outside and stroll, down the alley, up toward the big rock, over to the playground, the early chill rustling our fleece. We spend time on the swing, on the teeter-totter, but even the air and azure sky and the silver plane overhead can't settle your restlessness.

In a huff, you shuffle over to the huge red and yellow playground set, one of those dull, bleak monstrosities with too-safe rounded slides and padded walkways. But instead of going up, you go under—into the soft light between the grates, into the little cave under the equipment where it's even cooler and the sun won't shine. The wood chips here are cool and moist, resisting the warm day. You plop down and gather a pile of chips around your legs, find some rocks, peer up through the slates in the walkway, and finally, look at me.

What are you waiting for, Dada? I imagine you saying. So I get down on my hands and knees and crawl to you.

We are all, right now, living how we will be known. This

moment matters. As a stamp upon the great starlight, perhaps not so much, but when you woke miserable this morning and looked to me for that moment, the one that will make a difference, I didn't understand. And when I tried to calm you with action and movement, I didn't understand.

And as I scuttle under that plastic fort with you, it begins to register that every moment will matter, every day. Even those days when you think you know it all. Even those moments when I waver. For our tiny flash of life against the greater backdrop of everything, that's something to celebrate. We are all so small and yet we each can mean something so huge. That's pretty remarkable really, if we can just figure it out, and mostly that means just being.

Baby, we are cascading waterfalls, you and I and your mother, crashing and roaring; every day is full of grace and calamity, roar and peace. This week, you become what the books call a *toddler*. How can that be? My peanut. My tiny panda. And yet, just the other day, did you sit in your room by yourself, paging through a book? Was that you dancing to "Five Little Monkeys," a song I've heard so many times that my brain registers it as nothing more than white noise, except this one time, because you danced and patted your head and, my God, you pointed and wagged your finger when the doctor scolds the monkeys. I watch your face and your eyes as you absorb the world, information rushing in uninhibited because everything is new input, every word and sound. How it must feel to be at the edge of the universe like that, every waking moment a new moment! Every step is a step closer to understanding time itself, to being aware, to being a more powerful miracle. I can't keep up, baby, and I can't stop you either. Was that you, my tiny panda, who looked up at me and said, "Papa"?

And through all of that, there are days when you take flight, and there are days when you just want me to make it right.

Of long afternoons and early mornings reading Dr. Seuss over and over, of waking at 6:00 AM to your little face just inches from mine, of the strawberries you can now eat whole and the cookie jar you can now find. Of the beat-up cushion fort that I finally get to make with you and of the tiny tantrum you throw when it's time to leave.

I sit there in that cold playground and watch you watch me, and if I look closely enough, I can see the input now, the daily, hourly, minute-by-minute stream of wonderment and life that comes pouring in, unfettered. A crow outside our window, a new fruit—all equally tremendous, all fodder for this organic, living system of firing neurons and synapses, this soft bundle of stardust, this miracle. As we enter a new phase, this uproar called *toddler*, I continue to be utterly amazed.

I'm pulled out of my thoughts by a tug on my sleeve. You hand me a tiny rock and push a pile of wet chips my way and smile. This time, this moment, you're directing me. I pull some chips over my shoes and there we sit, protected, invisible, watching the adults with dogs, the too-loud teenagers, the little kids charging overhead, their tiny feet echoing down to our chamber. We are in the middle of the universe, my baby and me, surrounded yet alone. Just because you're so small, why would I think you couldn't have a bad day? Or a bad dream? Or just want to be alone for a little while?

Let the world do what it will. You and I, we'll just wait it out until you're ready. I'm glad you want me here to wait it out with you.

YELLOW CRAYON

On a recent book tour in my hometown of Buffalo, on a whim, I visit my mother's grave.

I was a rudderless young man when she passed, but her strength still gives me strength. And she's still present—in the diaries that describe her world travels, in the photos of her wide grin holding me on her knees, in the way my father looked at her.

Someday, baby, we'll talk about her, and I'll tell you how sometimes when I'm out there alone, or nervous, or anxious, I talk to her—that I have words now that I didn't or couldn't as a teenager.

Coming out here to a lonely cemetery alongside a busy highway is often about respecting loss, about coming to terms with those hard days, about figuring out a better way forward, and maybe bridging who I was with who I am.

I see those same echoes of motherhood in your mom, my wife.

The artist Sarah Walker once said that becoming a mother is like discovering the existence of a strange new room in a house where you already live. In other words, everything changes, everything stays the same. I don't have a whole lot to add to that; I miss my mom, I'm grateful you have an amazing mom. I feel like I can never do enough or say enough to thank them, and on and on.

And I wonder every day, would they have been friends, my mother and your mother? I'm pretty sure that they would be soldiers in motherly arms, sharing battle stories, having in common, perhaps, a depth of soul that would exist between them—having babies past and present to love. Would they explore that new, strange room together, locking the door behind them, sharing a space reserved only for them? I choose to believe yes.

The grandmother you'll never meet is one of many souls and lifetimes of love and knowledge and faith looking down on you, little one. Or around you.

There are so many in my life, including your grandmother, who never had a chance to meet you. So if all you are going to have of them is images and stories, then all you really have is us. We—meaning your mother and I—are the conduits through which time itself is to be filtered down to you. Or are we?

The ancient Greeks believed that the only constant was change and adding time to that change was simply a way of ordering that movement. You are young, time passes, and now you are old. But time itself, your position on the graph of life, is much fuzzier.

After all, even if she were to have survived to meet you, my mother of my timeline would have been different from the grandmother of yours. The grandfather you know now is not the same as the father your mother knew. There are only memories that connect you—us—to who we were and who you are.

This possibility gives me solace on those autumn afternoons when you explore a new corner of our yard or spin, heedless of direction, on our porch, and out of nowhere I realize that my mother missed you by thirty-five years. But she's in me and you have me and that means she's in you, too.

As I step out of the car at the cemetery, one of your crayons—yellow—rolls out onto the pavement, and I stare absently at it for a minute before placing it at my mother's grave. I'm not sure why. Maybe it's regret at the two souls never meeting, or sorrow at you having only pictures of one of your grandmas, or maybe it's a beginning.

Besides, I'm a storyteller. I don't have to think too hard to see the path ahead, now as clear as the yellow crayon against the marble marker—make one proud, make the other aware. I close my eyes, and for just a second, I picture you on my mother's knee. But it's just a moment; I'm done here.

And anyway, were my mom here, I know what she'd say— be careful on that step, baby, pull up your hood, it's chilly, and let me hear you howl like a wolf.

WHO ARE YOU?

In an unmowed field up in the northern mountains of our state, we find a vast field of wild strawberries. I tuck your pants into your socks, dab a little bug spray on your cuffs, and you totter off, a tiny creature just getting her feet under her there among the universe.

You yank a barely ripe berry off a twisted vine and mush it in your hands before dropping it. You try again, this time more gently, and the berry comes off whole.

And I think to myself, "who are you and how do you know?" I've been thinking a lot lately, baby, about what you might understand—about us, about your home, about a strawberry. Does it all bleed together into emotional peaks and valleys for you? Your belly full of juicy fruit, dancing with Mom, splashing in water, all good, and you cognizant of the joy those things bring you and therefore all equally desired?

The philosopher John Searle has suggested that the very fact of our consciousness is a function of biology. Consider that! Brain processes functioning not because of something, but just because; a light that shines simply because you are awake.

Not, "I think, therefore I am." But rather, "I am, therefore I am."

You are you, baby, because, well, because you are you. You are one of billions and billions of atoms—all identical—all raging through space and time, and yet—you are you alone, singular in your consciousness. All because you are alive.

Someday, perhaps, you will know that the strawberry is mentioned in ancient Roman literature, that fifteenth-century European monks used the strawberry as ink to illuminate their manuscripts, and that George Washington himself cultivated strawberries at Mount Vernon. But for now, you are just conscious of the juice that runs down your pink cheeks and the tart sting that causes you to smack your lips and the afternoons of rooting in the fields with your mother, shrieking every time another bright red berry peeks up out of the blades.

Recently, I came across a passage written by the great filmmaker Werner Herzog who said that "civilization is like a thin layer of ice upon a deep ocean of chaos and darkness." But what *is* civilization?

Is it the act of order, of discovering what makes you, you? Is it the language of you? The other day, I had a conversation with you, baby, a full on, "berries," "hungry dada," "mine," "all done" conversation about a snack of strawberries and cheese. Nineteen months into this journey, and we are talking. My daughter spoke to me. Is that not the very outline of the beginning of the start of the human experience, soon to be molded and expanded and too often twisted?

Or perhaps that's part of the darkness Herzog considers.

And the chaos? We like to think that we all come out of the gate with equal potential for understanding and greatness.

But maybe the chaos he speaks of suggests that we all don't share in equal opportunity and fortune, that not even communication can always keep the monsters away.

I choose instead to consider the ice—a mother and daughter sharing that deep green field, a vast chasm before them, bigger and deeper and stronger than anything mere mortal coils can withstand. And yet, are we not the ice? Is love not a bond, a language of a different sort? Maybe we are mere ice and maybe that makes all this that much more worthwhile. Where am I going with this? I'm not sure.

Listen more. In the face of such fragility, "hungry dada" takes on a weight as vast and deep and chaotic and dark as the ground under that field of berries. Ask yourself today, who are we? Then listen for the answer.

This, then, is all you, the same always, changing always, knowing and not, alive because you are. You are picking strawberries because you can, because maybe you—we all—are wired that way.

Maybe we should all be picking strawberries.

ELEPHANT DIRT

We are exhausted and filthy, and we both stink.

You cup your hands and dig into a thin layer of gravel, rocks, and dirt. We are high above the road in the White Mountains, on a rock outcropping called Elephant Rock. A sharp wind whips through Crawford Notch, shoots straight up the rock, and tussles your already wild and unruly wall of hair. We've been exploring the Appalachian Mountain Club's Highland Center area of the notch these past couple days, just you and me—dipping our feet into the muddy water, picking wildflowers in the fields near the center, crawling and climbing on any stable surface (and a few unstable ones).

Your mother and I want your connection with nature to be routine and regular; your sweat and mosquito bites ought to be every day, not just once in a while. Not just on vacation. When you were just six months old and barely crawling, we took you here, put you on the smooth granite, and stood back to watch you climb. We sunk you into the shallow mud of a stream and sat with you along the shore, the water bugs glimmering at your toes.

"Da!" you say. "Da!" Your eyes are clear, and you look up at me, showing me your fistfuls of dirt and twigs, and you roar like a tiny twenty-five-pound dinosaur, dumping the entire concoction into my outstretched hand.

This is our training. My training because I am growing soft and my knees have begun to plead with me daily. Your training because I want everything for you; in particular, I want you to be a child with perpetual dirt under your fingernails.

But whatever the results, the method will be you and me, with the rocks and sand under our feet and the wind in our hair. So we hike, little by little, inch by inch. First, little woods hikes like this—a round trip of about 0.7 miles up to this extraordinary lookout shaped like the head of an elephant about 600 feet above the notch that marks the entrance to Crawford.

And besides singing "The Wheels on the Bus Go 'Round and 'Round" about 1,000 times, you are perfectly at home on my back, patting the back of my head, saying "hat, hat" over and over at my bandana.

You appear to be perfectly suited for walking, my little imp, where those moments of connection begin to transcend routine, where we are removed from the everyday and flooded with existential input. Walking with you in a forest is an epiphany, where every leaf and rustle of a blade of grass becomes a healing salve. To connect, we disconnect.

Your fearlessness is daunting—steep cliffs, buzzing bees, mushrooms—none of those things appear to give you any pause at all, and we'll have to work on that some. But for now, we have this little summit to ourselves with no worries.

I'm not sure what you plan on building with your rocks, but you return with another load, stumble, and go down hard in the dirt. I move to sweep you up, but instead you just wipe your hands on your sweater and move on—focused, happy, disheveled, in the mountains.

ONE LEAF

There, among the millions of golden leaves, you stop in your tracks, select one on a pile of hundreds, and delicately pluck it off the mound.

"Leeefs," you say and hand it to me.

We are outside on a startling fall day strolling down a bike path near the Piscataqua River. This afternoon smells pure, a window between seasons, an escape hatch—too cool for sweat or bugs, to warm for a chill. You walk, then climb into the stroller, then walk again as you see fit. We have all the time in the world.

I tuck your leaf present into my pocket, and you smile and go back about the business of exploring. Times like these, baby, I think maybe you're the key to understanding the human condition. Let's not get all Hallmark about this and pretend we're going to face the world with child-like wonder and an appreciation for discovery. That's not it.

But why that one leaf? For millennia, babies have been left out of philosophical literature, but recently, psychologists like Alison Gopnik have begun suggesting that the depth of thought and reflection that goes on in the brains of toddlers is worthy of far deeper existential study than mere information input; that in fact, they are like little scientists, testing, creating scenarios, thinking about what happened and what might happen.

What will picking this particular leaf make dad do? Will he take it? Will he say it's dirty? What if I do the same for a stone? What if I put it in my mouth, or tear it?

What a revelation then, that little kids aren't chaotic, but rather hyper-focused, considering every action, deciphering scenarios like a World War II codebreaker. Try doing that in your everyday life for ten minutes. Look at your actions—even the most minor—as having consequences.

What will happen if you leave your house one minute earlier? What if you wear red instead of blue, eat an apple instead of a pear? What if you give a buck to that guy on the corner? What if you compliment a coworker you rarely speak to?

As adults, I fear this level of engagement and the ripple effect of constantly being present would drive us mad.

But baby, you just look up at a birdhouse off the side of the trail and laugh. You pick up a twig, study it, and fling it across the path. Finally, you settle on a tiny sliver of water pooling on the pavement. "Paaaaaa!" you shriek, using a shorter version of *pani*, the Nepali word you know to mean "water."

You touch the puddle with the tip of your finger, bring it toward your tongue, and look at me. I say, "No, Uma, yucky." You smile, rub your hands on your pants, and move on into the universe.

DELICATE LOCKS

With no restraint, your hair is nearly a caricature—a wall of curls and deep lines billowing about your head. Make no mistake, hair is hardly trivial—I should know, given my fleeting supply. Hair will play an enormous role in the childhood formation of your identity, and not just because yours is lovely. Pretty soon you're going to discover Rapunzel, and then maybe Samson, though the hair game tends to end up at Medusa's door every time.

There is, of course, an aesthetic philosophy of hair, a wildly subjective, culturally particular way to consider the subject. Is a good haircut timeless? Would an adult with your hair be thought beautiful, or mad? And what, if anything, do you think on those bath nights when a droplet of water drips from your hair to your nose and you roar with laughter?

I'm reminded of those pink-cheeked, curly-haired Renaissance babies, all doe eyes and fluttery. Art historian Matthew Averett wrote that middle-class Italian families around this time started finding themselves with enough expendable income to start paying for portraits of their kids—as opposed to the nearly exclusively Jesus man-baby paintings of the Middle Ages. And guess what? They wanted their babies to be beautiful.

Of course, that inclination toward beautiful babies continues to this day—the ultimate artistic endeavor, no? Is there anything we can create that we hold in higher regard? An organic, lifelong piece of performance art constantly evolving, adding, withdrawing. We create tiny curated museums to your life, in pictures and videos, through the years, digitally and on our own walls—each life, your life, baby, a years-long exhibition. And we invite other aficionados of BABY to explore our collection.

But right now, you know nothing of this. You just push a handful of your delicate, beautiful hair away from your eyes, and you turn toward me and bat those lashes, and I take another picture—another moment of stardust art captured for the ages.

FIRE

Baby, day to day with you is a slipstream of movement—a crashing wildfire of ecstatic, revelatory moments leaving a daily wake of new life, new breath, and new direction.

You burn white hot, every second a raging blaze of needs and input and love.

In one of those flow moments—indirect of purpose, unthinking, instinctual—you shift in my arms, and as I move to compensate, I feel the muscle in my lower back twist and pop, and a sharp ripple of pain leaves my lungs without air. Unthinking. My attempts to stem the river flow of life teaching me a lesson on the dangers of not being in the moment.

Or perhaps I'm just old.

Moments of pain, moments of insight and inspiration, moments of love so extreme, all answered often by tears. The pop philosopher Jason Silva has suggested that we rarely cry out of pure sadness, but because something is more beautiful than we expected it to be, the connection overwhelming our ability to mitigate the experience intellectually.

Gazing at the Grand Canyon the first time provides the same emotional explosion as watching you sleep, the infinite, incalculable mystery of time present in both—bringing tears out of simple wonder and awe. And maybe a thrown-out back as well.

Recently, a dear friend suggested that in writing about you, what I'm actually writing about is innocence.

The innocence of love? Is that not what everything is about, or should be? Perhaps I'm not breaking any new ground here at all, perhaps this has nothing to do with me or you. Maybe, when we are awake, when we are alive, when we have any breath left to give—even when our very muscles burn like fire—the answer is all around us all the time.

Is that too simple an answer, love? Too obvious? But when I'm next to you, little bean, there's nothing complicated at all about it. Even when you cry. Even when you drive me crazy. Even when you wake up at 2:00 AM. You are innocent. I love you. Does the fact of your innocence strengthen that love? Because if I answer that I'd love you no matter what, then I must love everyone—innocent or not—no matter what, right?

The great poet Rainer Maria Rilke had quite a bit to say about this. He believed that love itself was created for another—when we love someone, that love reconstructs us, makes us bigger. He said, "Love is a high inducement to the individual to ripen, to become something in himself, to become world for himself for another's sake, it is a great exacting claim upon him, something that chooses him out and calls him to vast things."

To become world for himself for another's sake; every moment that I sit and watch you eat, play with you, read books with you, and yes, change your diaper, I become a bigger world. Better and bigger even in the face of setbacks. Stronger, despite the knowledge that this will end someday. Inspired, despite or perhaps because I understand that time—if it is real at all—is fleeting.

If you can make me a world, can I be that *to* the world? I don't know. But at least now, because of you, I'm aware, acutely, sharpened, determined to try.

What then can we conclude about this innocent love? Only that the two of us, two worlds, are infinite in potential, exploding around and through and because of each other. Every moment is a miracle.

Where do we go from here—what comes next? Everything.

TENDRILS

On a cool winter night—the evening of Solstice—you slip into the corner of our sofa under the lights from the Christmas tree, pull up the light purple blanket your grandmother created for you, and tuck a corner under your chin.

On either end of our sofa is a blanket made by her: one with the English alphabet, the other adorned with the Nepali alphabet. I marvel at the deep connection spanning two generations of this most simple and evolutionary act of creation.

The writer and philosopher David V. Ciavatta wrote that family heirlooms serve as a crucial symbol of the durability and sustainability of a family's spirit and of the perspective a family leaves on the world.

In other words, baby, we are only flesh and heartbeats, but these small tokens—as meaningless as they may seem to those outside the family line—serve as invaluable waymarks along the generational road to create and sustain and strengthen your identity.

Remember those thin, timeless fibers I always talk about, the tendrils connecting us to each other? Well, here are two, little bean, straight down the line, a direct path from your grandmother's hands to yours. And like the fibers that make up those blankets—thin, delicate, impermanent—perhaps they will all fall away someday like a sand mandala, and all that will be left is the sharp turns of those soft letters in the memory of your fingertips and the warm protective embrace of the quilt against your skin on a chilly evening. And you'll remember those heirlooms and the love of your grandmother, and maybe, just maybe, you'll start to think about what you'll pass down to your own grandchildren, what spirit of your family you'll continue.

Perhaps the magic will be what holds. Perhaps the gifts, or maybe even the tree.

During this time of connection, when winter had its strongest influence on the frozen landscape, Germanic Norse pagans would bring entire evergreen trees into their homes. It was believed that the spirits of these massive yule trees would inhabit their homes and bless the inhabitants. The needles and cones would be burned as incense—smoke and fragrance filling the home with the protective spirit-magic of the evergreen.

Those long-forgotten traditions born out of both practicality and terror of the cold northern European winter feel present and immediate, baby, as you embrace our tree (your second, but your first with comprehension). I imagine how magical this must be to you, how otherworldly.

The deep groves of holiday tradition are burned into human-kind's DNA—whether Diwali or Christmas or Ramadan or Hanukkah or your birthday. I think of a two-year-old child, layered in wool and fur, the deep aroma of fir swirling through her home, her parents asking the tree for blessing and protection, this symbol of life towering over her, a living yuletide god.

And I can't help thinking how hundreds of years and

thousands of miles and generations of conflicting culture and time itself may separate you, but for a split second, in your eyes, twinkling there beside our own tree, she is you and you are her.

She is you and you are her, there beneath your grandmother's blanket. So cuddle up, my child, lay back and tuck those edges around your little toes and know that you're safe in time, and safe now in the shadow of the yule.

year three
METAL

LIGHT OF THE MIND

Today, you woke me up with, "Good morning, Daddy. Wake up. Get up." Three sentences, complete, with a call to action and thought-driven outcome.

Yesterday, you used a conjunction, "because." As you might imagine, I've been keeping track of these linguistic leaps—how amazing to hear the complexity of speech and language develop.

"Why did you drop that?" you were asked.

"Because I didn't want it on the table." Conjunction. First-person pronoun. Contraction. Question answered. A bit of attitude.

Language, said John Stuart Mill, is the light of the mind. I watch that light shine in you, baby, burning like a candle, flaring every so often like a sparkler, snuffed out now and again and replaced with grouchy grousing. Your words are becoming you, and you are reflected in your language. You speak, therefore you are. In a world that sometimes feels like it's designed to put out the flame, I hope your fire continues to burn.

Still, every day now, I feel like I just can't keep up, like I'm running along a shore trying to keep pace with the flow of the river after a spring thaw. But here's the thing—I'm going to run out of shore long before the end of the river. At some point

I'll just have to find a comfortable spot of grass and sit down and watch you go, baby, watch your flow.

But that day is not today. Today, I shake the sleep out of my eyes and lift my creaky bones out of bed and let you take me.

Get up. It *is* a good morning. Go!

METAL

As the setting sun begins to fire up the endless Indiana sky, we are on the prowl for the human tooth rock. Made famous by a dentist in Elkhart, the concrete rock contains thousands of pulled teeth, and it rests, apparently, at a downtown museum.

We are tooling through the upper Midwest; the days are long, the car is loaded with snacks, and the possibilities are—as always—endless.

But the museum is closed, permanently it seems, and no amount of peering over the tall wooden fence allows me to see the rock. I walk back to the rest stop where you and your mother are taking a break, dejected to have wasted time looking for something so frivolous and in vain, as it turns out.

But as I turn to head back, I hear, "Daddy, Daddy, an orange moose!"

You are running, eyes as lit as the sun, skipping, pointing. There is no moose, but it is still grand and definitely orange. I lift you up onto the back of the shimmering elk and you squeal, your shriek of joy echoing off the old walls of the closed museum.

And as the big sky sun collapses into the surrounding corn fields and creates a Rorschach test out of the billowing clouds, I take a deep breath and inhale this unexpected moment, this glorious, warm few seconds in the middle of nowhere, holding you, my girl, there atop the orange elk.

* * *

In a small tree-lined playground near the Fox River, we find an abandoned football. You make a beeline for the basketball court, the football tucked under your arm like you're the littlest running back.

And we play catch—or a slightly stunted version of catch where you sort of throw the ball as hard as you can, and I try to scoop it up off the pavement and underhand roll it back to you. This goes on for a long time, broken only by your occasional attempts to catch squirrels and a great deal of laughter.

You, your mother, and I are in Green Bay, and at some point, as the sun begins to drop to the west, I can see the distant glimmer of Lambeau Field—no need to be a sports fan to appreciate the storied history of that gridiron.

So here we are, little one, rolling across America, devouring cheese curds and chili popcorn, bathing in corn dust and Lake Michigan sand, asking truckers to honk and drinking the worst possible truck stop coffee the highway has to offer.

The miles roll by, and we content ourselves with gourds and tomatoes and fridge magnets and cardboard signs that insist you stop to see the world's biggest. When it's light out, you gaze out your car window and count the red barns, and when it's dark, you tell me, "Drive faster, Daddy, don't let the moon catch us."

And now we are playing catch at dusk on a raggedy concrete court. A train horn howls in the distance like a wolf and our fingernails are filthy and one of your pigtails is crooked; I think that maybe life is perfect.

You sit back and spin the ball; we watch it turn and rock and finally stop. We all laugh, and you say, "I think I'd like a pear."

So we eat a pear and drive and the road lifts us up; there is so very much to love.

* * *

In an enormous city park along the shore of the St. Mary's River, you are so eager to play that you push against my arms, barely even out of the car. The massive metal playground structures are scattered under the trees like blistering suns, their gravitational pull too great for you to resist.

We are in Sault Ste. Marie, across from Canada and just up shore from Lake Superior. The sky and water are brilliant blue, the air is mild, and the day is ours. It's too late in the season for campers and too early for ice. I'm delighted to discover that the shimmering metallic playground equipment appears to date from around the time I was your age.

There is a steel whirligig worn smooth by decades of little hands holding on for dear life. There's a two-story slide rocket ship with metal bars, and I have to help you up the ladder, standing under you as you go. When we are seated in the capsule, we blast that puppy off and land on the moon.

And there are cartoon character teeter-totters so old and used that Yogi Bear looks like one of those post-apocalyptic characters—is he smiling or crying?

If you look hard enough at these structures, you can see

back in time. They are a looking glass—the indents and curves of the seats, the handles shining bright silver and worn to the steel, the deep grooves under the swings. This is so unlike our sanitary plastics of today's harmless playground. I close my eyes and listen for the laughter of ghost children.

After a spell, we run down to the shore to join your mother who has collected sparkling rocks, shells, twigs, and shimmering stalks of algae which she fashions into shore art. You strip off your shoes and socks and wade into the chilly water, a slight northern wind mussing your hair.

I watch from a rise as an enormous cargo ship barrels down, down from the locks north of us and chugs by only a few hundred yards from where you stand. The boat blows its whistle, low and deep, and we can feel the sound vibrating under our feet.

You look up, but only for a moment. The smooth pebbles under your toes are far more interesting than any mere thousand-foot vessel.

I slip off my own shoes and join you in the water just as the ripples from the ship begin to lap up against our knees and our feet sink deeper into the cold sand. The ship's whistle sounds again, this time distant, saying goodbye. You dip your hand deep into the sloshing river and retrieve a palm-sized black stone, a perfect sphere.

You search for a pocket, find none, shrug, and heave the stone back into the river where it will once again begin its 10,000-year journey back to shore.

EVERY TIME

Today, for the first time in our short journey together, you play on the big girl swing—the one without the bucket or the oversize seat. It doesn't last long—a few nervous minutes of my hovering over you as you learn to kick your legs and hold on at the same time. You swing for a few seconds, then decide the big green seat is more your speed.

Did you know, baby, that it was your sister city—Manchester, England—that first introduced self-contained public playgrounds all the way back in 1859?

These moments come so fast now that I'm certain I'm missing them, partially because the most significant moments are usually the most normal.

For example: yesterday, you sat at the kitchen table and ate cereal. Cheerios. In a bowl. With milk. You ate it with a spoon.

And just the other day, after school, apropos of nothing, you simply recited the Pledge of Allegiance to me. My jaw dropped. It still takes some getting used to the idea that only a fraction of your daily input —which is so large now—is coming from me or your mother.

All this other information is pouring in every second that you're awake. This is impossible for an adult to conceive—we're already so packed with the commonest of information, knowledge that is so base and matter of fact that it doesn't even feel like knowledge.

Next time I write my name, I'll try to be mindful that at some point, I didn't know how to do that. Or open the fridge. Or turn on a faucet. Input, it's all input. And you, baby, are the great receiver now.

As hard as this is for me to say, baby, don't wait for me. Don't slow down. Don't let me or anything hold you back. Take it all in and keep moving forward.

Just know that if you need a rest, if you need advice, or if you just need a bowl of Cheerios, your old man is going to be right behind you with an empty bowl and a gallon of milk—every single time.

GROTTO CHILD

It's late—we should be winding down, but you're full of energy. I'm folding clothes when you jump up on the bed and crawl into the laundry basket. Used to be you could sleep in there. Now, alas, your feet hang over the side—I'm marking your growth by the perimeters of a cheap green plastic laundry basket.

"Cover me, Daddy," you say, and I suddenly have one of my brilliant ideas of the variety that usually gets me in trouble.

You can't sit up in the basket horizontally, but you still can vertically. So I prop it vertically against the bed's backboard, pile cushions on either side, and toss a blanket over the top, forming a sort of play grotto. You crawl in giggling even before the structure is finished.

"Cover me!" you squeal again.

So I grab a quilt, brace it up top, and fold it down over the opening. Further expanding upon my brilliance, I run and get you a headlamp and turn off the lights.

"Now you're a cave explorer!" I say.

My spelunker. My grotto child. My baby Lady of Guadalupe.

As you laugh and play in your laundry basket grotto fort, I begin feeling wistful. These moments now, of you internalizing your learning, are growing more frequent and stronger. This is good, I know. This is normal, I know.

David Sobel of Antioch University New England literally wrote the book on kids and forts. In it he writes that fort building for kids is a form of explorational development and the first inklings of independence and a place to call their own.

"A fort is, literally and figuratively," he writes, "a defense against all the forces of the outside world."

But just as the melancholy begins to take hold, I hear you from behind the quilt. "Daddy, come in, come in!"

I can barely fit my head and shoulders in there with you, but that's good enough.

"Do you like your cave, baby girl?" I ask.

"No, Daddy, it's a rocket ship, ready for blast off!"

"Oh! Okay! Where are we going?"

"Starbucks, Daddy, we're going to Starbucks."

And so my baby astronaut and I lift off to seek espresso and cake pops, and as we orbit the earth, just her and I alone among the stars, I'm grateful that at least today, she needed a copilot dad for her rocket ship fort.

FEARLESS

Why are you fearless? I certainly am not. That's from your mother, I suspect.

When you were six months old and you wanted your little panda stuffed bear, you managed to crawl halfway across the room to get it, oblivious to the fact that you simply should not have been able to do that.

In Turkey and India, you walked, you bit into limes and oranges. "No, I can do it," I hear more and more now. "No, I can do it."

This is no humblebrag, baby. More like I'm terrified.

You are the embodiment of Bia, the great Titan goddess of energy and force—immovable, stubborn. In images she is winged and fierce, head up, holding a scepter or spear or sword. Hair a mad storm of clouds and curls. Her mother is the goddess Styx, the one whose name is evoked over solemn oaths. Ovid writes that whenever a god or goddess takes an oath, water from the River Styx is fetched in a golden pitcher/cup, and the oath-taker slowly pours out the water while pronouncing the oath.

Heavy stuff, baby. But I am not Zeus nor Mercury, and certainly no Apollo. Maybe Sancus, the Roman God of Loyalty? Boring but consistent, at least.

In a park nearby—or any park—you don't play, you attack

the plastic and metal, and it's all I can do to find a place to catch you if you fall. I struggle with this, baby, much as I did a few years ago with your bigger sister as we climbed mountains. All those Band-Aids, all that ice on sore muscles and tape that wrapped feet and ankles. Every wound you receive, I feel too.

For now, you expend enough energy to go around, so I work to feed off that, to give me inspiration and strength. I do love watching you run. Someday though, maybe soon, I am not going to be able to keep up, and someday you are not going to care if I do or don't. Someday. But not today.

Today, my tiny Bia, just explode like a supernova and don't worry about me. I can watch, I can give you a boost, a foot up for that extra few inches. I may not be able to keep up, but I can't be burned either.

SOME MORNINGS/SOME EVENINGS

Some mornings, the house is cold and the sun is too low and the wind outside seems to seep through the rafters like sand trickling through an open hand.

Some mornings begin with regret—regret at not having worked enough, read enough, played enough, ate right, exercised. Not having done the dishes the night before.

Some mornings, when I open the drapes in your room and there is no sun and clouds hang like dirty cotton, you roll over and say, "No, Daddy, no, I'm tired."

Some mornings I'm tired too, and we're late, and I think I can be stubborn as well. Sometimes I think I deserve to be stubborn.

Some mornings come after early mornings where you call out in the middle of the night and I don't know why, and I'm exhausted, but your mother or I take you and pat your belly and we all just sniffle through the dark.

And some mornings, I know you have an ear infection, and I know you can't understand that I'm doing everything I can to make the pain go away and I'm frustrated and short with you, and that makes it worse.

Some mornings I forget that you may be little, but you are allowed to feel awful. You may be little, but you have bad nights as well. You may be little, but innocence does not always equate to happiness.

I'm sorry when I forget that. Some mornings I am badly flawed.

But in the end, we come together—irritable, but together.

Some mornings do not end upbeat or settled. Some just end with an unspoken agreement to try again the next morning, and the next.

Some mornings, after you leave, I miss you. All mornings actually.

* * *

Later that evening, we try something new: an anything evening. Your ears are still ringing, the rain outside won't end.

So we give you anything you want. One full evening doing anything that falls within the laws of physics and doesn't include ice cream. Tonight, we say, is your night. What do you want?

"My cups," you say.

"Okay."

"Ice cubes."

"Fine."

"Paint!"

I can see where this is going. But okay, it's what you want.

So we get a big play tray, lay out some towels and napkins, give you a selection of paint and some brushes, and we are off to the anything evening races.

I give you a bucket of ice cubes, but you ask for the ice cube tray as well, so you get that too. And we let it be, just move away, give you space, don't wipe up when you spill, don't try to stop you from eating the paint. If you ask for more, you get it.

And so it goes. Confronted with no barriers—except perhaps the buckles of your highchair and your own imagination—the ice cube tray soon becomes a palette, with each melting ice cube getting a touch of a different color or combination until all sixteen cube pockets are a slightly different shade.

This isn't reinventing the wheel, of course; play anything days are becoming more common. We're glad to see it works, at least this time, restoring some equilibrium to an otherwise shaky day.

The journalist Paul Sloane has suggested there are two main reasons why children are more creative than adults. One is because they have not yet learned what they can't do, therefore anything is possible.

The other is because they tend to receive much more positive reinforcement for their creativity than adults. If your three-year-old tells you a story about a yellow zucchini elephant riding a rocket ship made out of strawberries to the moon, we call that imagination. If an adult told you that story, you'd put your head down and walk away quickly.

As you're mixing your ice cube colors and begin painting your face, I resist the urge to clean you up and consider how utterly caged in we adults often are. Why isn't anything possible to us? Why don't we lavish more positive energy onto each other?

"Daddy, more ice cubes please."

I bring out another tray, but as I get ready to pour them into the bucket, you say, "No, no, break them into pieces."

I do.

"Now, put each piece in a different tray."

"How many?" I ask looking at the bucket of two dozen ice cube pieces.

"All of them!"

"Anything you want, baby girl, anything you want."

RUMBLE ON

The first time you met your cousins—my nephews—baby, our pictures were primarily of you being held in their laps. Now, well, let's just say it's hard to get a quiet shot of you with them because the first thing you want to do is wrestle. Roughhouse.

This speaks volumes, of course, about where your head space is—comfortable enough with the boys, safe at your aunt's house, taught well enough to not be a wallflower.

But really, I can't say enough about my nephews. They are tough guys, athletic. I've never seen elementary kids eat so much. They are gentle, but they don't pull their punches. They let you climb the stairs, but they stay close to catch you if need be. And you are a handful, but the oldest, Ben, displays a level of patience that extends well beyond his age.

The day of Thanksgiving prep churns on. We all stay close to home; a big plastic railway set is brought up from the basement, and you love the remote-control car—in particular the fact that you can make the cat chase the car.

Life proceeds as it should—the kids get older, the adults get grayer, things are forgotten from the grocery, other things are spilled, the house gets messy then clean, then messy again; coffee mugs and pint glasses pile up. And outside, the first few swirling snowflakes fall.

My dad, your grandpa, isn't here to partake this year, but

if he was, nothing would change. He'd just be in the corner and life would revolve around him. In fact, he'd be mortified to discover that anything different happened once he was no longer with us. So we'll continue much like we always have.

But now, baby, you can wrestle. And now the boys are young men. Now, leaving will be harder for you, and returning will be that much more anticipated.

And so the week rolls on, baby. Routine sets in fast here with you among your favorite people. You begin to sleep at the same time, wake at the same time. You watch your cousins and eat what they eat. Play like they do.

We all go to a giant playground center in the mall, and for three straight hours—punctuated only by water breaks—you slip and slide and run. We need to take turns watching you. By the end, my knees are red and bruised from following you through spaces too tight for me to walk.

There is no end to your energy.

Your mother grew up surrounded by four older boy cousins, and I begin to see echoes here—an unwillingness to be the smallest or the slowest.

Stubborn? Independent? Those both can go either way, strength like that can work for or against you. I'm beginning to understand that, perhaps, our role here is to build the foundation; the house, though—well, that'll be up to you. I can only hope there's enough room in it for us to visit sometimes.

You just keep firing, baby, keep moving and learning. Now is the time, here is the place.

SUSTAIN

On a recent trip to Buffalo to visit your cousins, we pack the boys into the car (you call them "The Boys") and prowl the streets in search of tacos. This has become something of a tradition, or perhaps a way of life is more accurate.

And no Taco Bell for us. Your mother—through the magic of the internet—has discovered a glorious hole in the wall, complete with a cardboard mariachi band in the window and ice cold Jarritos for the taking.

We push all our chairs together and sit elbow to elbow, a dozen enormous tacos between us, and feast until grease drips down our wrists and the chili peppers redden our cheeks, and finally you perform the grand finale of the evening, baby, with an acrobatic spill of horchata that results in a full-on mop-and-bucket episode and a series of sincere apologies. In other words, a good time.

The Dutch writer and academic Louise Fresco talks about food not in terms of nutrients and calories, but rather as a holy act. "It's about sharing. It's about honesty. It's about identity," she writes.

Many cultures regard cooking as a holy experience, and I'm fond of the idea that eating together is an act of honesty. So much happens during these moments, so much expression and connection. I suspect what Fresco means is that these can be moments in our lives where pretense can be allowed to drop and where listening becomes a positive trait.

And so much of that is gone, now, in a time of speed.

I know you don't think much of any of that, baby. You're hungry, you're with The Boys. I let you take a sip of my sweet soda, and the lights and colors shimmer and glow around you.

There is absolutely nothing special about this act, a play that is performed millions of times a day, in a million places, with a million different people and a million types of different foods. But this act being common is what elevates the experience into the realm of the sacred.

I know what you're thinking, baby. Is every hard-boiled egg a sacred moment, every slice of pizza, every cookie stolen from the countertop in the middle of the night? Maybe. Maybe it is.

But certainly tonight—tacos with a dear friend, two nephews, my daughter, and my wife—well, if that's not holy, then I don't know what is.

IMPROVISATION

I've been thinking a lot about music, baby. When you were still in your mom's belly, we'd listen to Dylan and the Beatles and Miles Davis. Three years later, you still perk up at the sound of a trumpet or saxophone. You even own a little plastic horn, yellow and orange and green.

In a month, you'll begin attending dance classes (I could have sworn you were crawling last week).

But your exposure and love of music came into better definition for me over the weekend when a friend with grown kids of his own asked me how fatherhood was, and all I could think to say was "amazing."

"Yeah," he said, "but amazing every day in a different way, right?"

Yes, of course! Like jazz, baby.

You are a solo, you are improvisation.

You are a John Coltrane riff suddenly exploding in my ears.

You are the smooth ecstasy of Art Blakey.

You are the famous Benny Goodman Carnegie Hall Concert when you blow so loud and I think the ceiling will fly off and the neighbors will run into the street yelling.

You are Wes Montgomery, coming in low and quiet when I least expect it.

And yeah, you are Miles Davis in his early seventies acid

funk stage where you are just doing your thing and I have no idea what's happening, but hey, it's your thing and you own it and I respect that.

Every day with you—sometimes many times a day—is something exquisite and new; is something terrifying and calamitous. Sometimes you are accessible, and everybody gets you. Sometimes only your mother or I get it. Other times, baby, you are flying solo, and we mere mortals are just along for the ride.

When you are off your game, you're still unique. And when you're good—when the moon is as perfectly round as your eyes and you reach for the ceiling and stomp your feet—the world bends its ear to listen to you.

During those times, you are divine revelation.

THERE IS NO END

On a cool, overcast evening, I pick you up from school, and you say, "Daddy, can we see scary Santa?"

You are referring to the curious Manchester landmark, a makeshift plastic enormous Santa set up next to a local Christmas tree lot. The Santa is an annual tradition in these parts.

You've already seen him, of course, many times. You've patted his grotesque belly, you've squealed in delight at his crazy eyes and the illumination of multicolored lights wrapped around his waist and neck. He makes no sense, contextually. You barely know what Santa is.

But we go. We go because you are so funny. I drive out of the way, we park, I carry you, and there we are again near a big intersection on a cold night, in front of a giant chipped and mangled plastic abomination. And you laugh. We go because you laugh.

Because I would drive until I ran out of gas and carry you for a hundred more miles to hear your laugh.

This journey we're on—the three of us—sometimes feels entirely external, like it's all and only about putting out energy. Giving it away, all of it, constantly, endlessly. And when I'm the most exhausted at 2:00 AM and you call, there's just more there to give away. It's just there.

It's wondrous.

Like how the ancients must have thought of lightning. Or what a fairgoer in 1900 must have thought of a light bulb. And I think, maybe, I have begun to understand a tiny bit.

Your grandfather would sit at the table with me sometimes, and I'd talk to him about my life and show him new technology on my smartphone—email, pictures, videos, websites. All those apps. Literally my whole life fitting into the palm of my hand.

But he wouldn't be amazed. He wouldn't marvel at how it all works. He'd shake his head and say, "Yeah, but can you make a phone call?"

He meant, don't forget the simple things, the original things. It's not complex, or at least, it does not have to be. And also, you don't have to understand everything.

So where are we now, baby? Hurtling through the cosmos, us three, just stardust particles, microscopic in the universe of the universe. Less than a fraction of a blink.

Will you, someday, long after I'm gone—when you're living in a world I cannot even begin to imagine today—read these notes and understand anything? Am I even making sense?

I'll try.

There is no end, in depth and strength, to how much I love you. Every moment, I love you more than I have loved you a day earlier. And every day, I know I am loving you less than I'll love you tomorrow.

To be clear, in case I somehow haven't been, this will be the case until I whisper my final breath.

There are a lot of scary Santas out there. There is so much life constantly whirling around us, so many places we can go, so much food. So many creatures. So much music. Endless forts to construct. Vegetables to plant. Books to read. Dances to learn. Hats to wear. Shoes and knees to scuff, mud to splash and snow to pack. We'll try to do it all, really, all of it.

Until then, I'll keep writing and your mother will keep being insanely strong and you'll keep laughing.

The world will cascade through time, baby, like it always does, and with a little luck, we won't even notice because we'll have too much to see.

year four
WATER

TINY DANCER

This morning, you begin ballet—your first class. My tiny dancer.

Your mother dresses you in a pink leotard with a ruffled tutu, and at school where you'll take your class, I take my time tying your ballet shoes.

I'm moving in a daze because it occurs to me that time has no meaning, isn't linear. I know this because suddenly I can feel the slates of the wooden rocking chair in the maternity ward pressing up against my back as I rocked you on the day you were born, as surely as I can feel the quilt of my deathbed in a final warm embrace.

And in between is you, the new dancer. You, crawling for the first time and you, running, and then riding, and then you, walking away. And you, spinning in ballet shoes that don't quite fit.

I hold your hand until the last possible moment because you are the tether to this revelation—when we are connected, I feel it all at once.

And I try to hold on by thinking of the awe of the ordinary. Earlier that morning, you asked me for a Tic Tac—you know I keep some in the car. I said yes, and you became so excited, kicking your little feet, clapping your hands. And I thought, what is THAT like? Being so full of joy and expectation at something like a tiny mint.

But that mindfulness is energy, and that energy our connection. Today, I'll consider ways the day will bring me the joy of your connection. Watching a pigeon in the parking lot, or the way a sweater feels on my skin, or the taste of water.

I'll pull way back. A perfect cup of coffee. A passing cloud. Sun on the top of my head. I'll go smaller. The smooth feel of a rock on my fingertips. A deep breath. The darkness behind my closed eyes. Even more. I'll sit down for ten seconds. Tighten my shoelaces. Touch the tip of a pencil.

I'll eat a Tic Tac.

We do these things every day, hundreds upon thousands of times. Today, I won't allow them to be basic. Today, as you dance, I'll make them remarkable.

Then you slip away, slip out of my hand, to dance, and I walk back to the car through the slush, and go home and sip coffee and write. And the world is the same. But I'm not.

BATTERED, SWOLLEN, AND CHASED AWAY

Few adventures are able to recover from "and then the hornets arrive," but all things considered, we came out relatively unscathed.

With you home for summer break and Mommy off to work, we decide this morning is going to be a full-on treasure hunting day full of jewels and flowers and excitement. We don't know that the excitement part will turn out to be easy!

We map out three geocaches to go after—all in the area of a commercial strip—figuring if it gets too hot, we can always take cover in some air-conditioned box stores.

The first cache is a bust, buried someplace perhaps in high weeds, and with a noisy lawn mower at our back, we hoof it over to Bass Pro Shop to pet the creepy stuffed animals and watch the sad fish.

Cache number two is near Walmart and is a big success—a green covered case hidden behind a light post. You grab a light blue jewel and find two sweet necklace blocks, one with the letter U. You even leave two of your own jewels and a little toy roller skate.

Cache three is supposed to be behind the Irving gas station, and it may be there for all we know. One of our rules of cache finding, baby, is to never stick our hands into any hole without first shining a light into it—a rule that you forget today.

I catch you just as you are about to plunge your little hand into a guardrail crevasse, but not soon enough. As I put my hand over yours to pull you away, the first hornet nails me on my left pointer finger knuckle, and then all hell breaks loose.

Our saving grace, I think, is that they are just as confused as we are as they come pouring out into the sweltering heat. I pull you up over the guardrail—not terribly gently, I must confess—holding you in front of me and turning my back to the swarm. I feel a second hit on my index finger, right above the already swelling knuckle, and two or three pelting my cap and backpack.

I just put my head down and run, clasping you, my hornet-agitating daughter, in front of me, my hand over your face. I hightail it around a turn and keep on running until we get into the gas station to assess the damage.

Damage seems minimal, another small nick on the back of my neck. But you have come out unscathed. Seems like the swarm had little interest in us once we started to run.

"Daddy, I don't like bees!" you say. Then, after we buy a packet of cherry Tic Tacs to celebrate our survival, "Can we find more treasure?"

And so we do. With my itchy neck and swollen hand, we decide that one out of three is a lousy success record, and we need to find one more to even the score. We locate it near Stark Park, a tiny pill container hidden behind a jumble of rocks. This time we both are very careful before retrieving it, though a bit sad to discover no treasure in the container beside a logbook.

"Sorry, Boo," I say, "no toys in there."

Without a sound, my little adventurer, you open your Hello Kitty treasure box and retrieve one of the little letter squares we found earlier.

"Put this in," you say. And so, there on the grass, sweating from the blistering heat, battered, bruised, and chased off but still standing, you, my little trooper, drop a toy in the container for the next kid to find.

Later that evening, you hold up my swollen hand and say, "Don't move." I hear you in the kitchen, and you return with an ice cube. "Here, Daddy."

"Thank you, baby, that feels much better."

We'll take it.

MADMEN AND WARRIORS

In a front yard cemetery where plastic skeletal hands burst up from plastic RIP graves, you approach a terrifying, slow-moving nun. She is cloaked in black, her hands horribly deformed, her face a smear of white paint and sunken eyes. She turns her head toward you in slow motion, stoops down to eye level, and says, "Well, what have we here?"

You don't even flinch. You hold your treat bag in front of you like a sword, like the pounds of sugar are a shield, like you are a fairy that slays evil nuns. You yell "Trick or treat," and it's a hex. A curse. A rejoinder that you have arrived to claim this Day of the Dead as your own, as only a child can.

I watch this transaction with acute interest—innocent fairy and fallen nun—on this day when the boundaries between the dead and the living are thin as tissue paper, and I'm lost in a haze of melancholy, of memories of the souls who will be remembered in the days ahead and of the fortunes foretold in the divinations of the little kids wandering the neighborhood dressed as madmen and warriors.

I'm grateful to Halloween as the herald of the great ask, to begin at the beginning—start with life, collapse into dust and then return to life.

In the Book of Wisdom, the part of the Bible traditionally used during the commemoration of All Souls' Day, there's a line that goes something like this: "In the memory of virtue, there is immortality."

In the contest of virtue, little one, even the evil nun can't break you. You smile, she laughs, she gives you an extra piece of candy, and all the skeletons clap their hands and the lost souls are found and the air crackles with immortality.

We are all lost, we are all found. We tremble in the night and find comfort in the light— where the glow of the orange, flickering Halloween lanterns reflects off shiny candy wrappers and sets your eyes on fire.

B.I.N.G.O.

We're on a quick run to Walmart, ostensibly to pick up some canned goods for a school donation drive—an opportunity, one supposes, to create a lesson in compassion out of the least compassionate place on earth.

You have questions. Why doesn't the family have food? Do they live outside? Can we buy them ice cream?

I don't have all the answers, but as we work our way down the canned goods aisle and pick up some orange slices, peas, and carrots (you want to take them all down off the shelf yourself), we reach some conclusions. Some families have less things than we do. Having more things is not always good. Sharing, however, is good.

And so it goes.

But this is Walmart, and despite my valiant attempts to distract you long enough to escape without going into *that* corner of the store, literally no one can miss the giant floor-to-ceiling balloon Santa or the holiday archway, and then, of course, the Christmas trees.

You are shaking, pleading with me. So we leave the cart and I let you lead me.

Honestly, I don't care. The trees look pretty. There's glitter everywhere. I'm certain that before we leave, we'll hear John Lennon's "Happy Xmas," and that will be fine. You're happy and that means I'm happy, and I know it's Walmart, but so what?

We get sidetracked at the end of the ornament aisle when, in your excitement to show me a gigantic stuffed teddy bear, you accidentally push the emergency exit door bar and a shrieking monkey alarm scares both of us into near paralyzation.

"Run!" I say. But we can't get far, and after a round of apologies where the bored clerk barely looks up from his register to assure us that it happens all the time, we ditch the Christmas section and make a beeline for the toys where we nearly get run over by a kid about your age blowing past us on a bright red tricycle.

His mom follows behind, and as she passes, she gives me that certain parental look—like a sort of shrug with her face that says, "What can you do?"

You look at me. You look at him. You look at me again.

"Go on," I say. What can you do?

I fasten a bright pink helmet on your head. We pick out the exact same tricycle, you pack a stuffed dog you have just now named B.I.N.G.O. into the trunk of the bike, and I set you free.

And I don't care, and neither do you. Nor does the other mother as she and I chase you two around the aisles. Her son is laughing and you're roaring, and even the Walmart staff look at us and walk a little faster in the other direction. Some shoppers applaud and you crash into somebody's leg, but this is Ben Hur now, and it's incumbent upon them to get out of your way.

You fly around a corner singing, "There was a farmer, had a dog and B.I.N.G.O. was his name," and we all scream, "Oh!"

Suddenly, there is magic happening, right there, in a place where magic isn't supposed to happen. And I want you to hold on to this, hold on as tight as you can to the moments when nothing else matters.

Because on the other side of town, not far from where you go to school, there's a family that needs canned corn. And nobody can predict what will happen next. So do what you can, little girl; help and sing and push those pedals hard and find joy anywhere. And give joy too.

WHAT WILL YOU BECOME?

As the adults gather before the ceremony, you run back and forth over the cushions and blankets, quivering with excitement. Your grandparents are here for Dashain, the Nepali high holiday—the victory of light over dark—a multi-day celebration deeply rooted in the Hindu Nepalese experience and celebrated by their diaspora around the globe.

But you, little one, you know nothing of Durga's great battle or that your aunt sowed the barley seeds herself days earlier to make jamara for the ceremony, or of the sacrifices, or the kites, or the bamboo swings, or the sacred rites.

No, you know only this: that you are the youngest and your grandfather is the oldest, and that distinction alone makes you both special. You two are the beginning and the end, the book ends of the family. You sit down on a cushion opposite him and clasp your hands together to receive tika. Even at this young age, you understand some part of what it means to use ritual to connect across time with those you have lost and to celebrate with those you have now.

As you two begin, I think, what will you become?

In Istanbul, we paused with you in the Hippodrome of Constantinople, now a bustling thoroughfare, to listen mesmerized to the call to prayer as it rang out into the ancient city. Then we set you down on the cool marble floor of Hagia

Sophia to wander on hands and knees where for a millennium and a half sultans and bishops held court.

At Thanksgiving, you sit next to your cousins and recite grace, and at Christmas we pass oplatki, but in the tradition of my father and mother, instead of wishing remembrance for loved ones, we break the wafer and wish those next to us peace, long life, and happiness.

At Easter we paint eggs. Before entering your great grand-mother's house for the first time, your aunt took you for a blessing before the house alter. You have twirled in front of a traditional Sufi whirling dervish. You have taken your first bites of solid food in a Pasni ceremony surrounded by family in a neighborhood temple near Lake Michigan in Chicago.

In our own backyard, you bring beads and acorns to our concrete Buddha. And in a garden at Arrowhead, the home where Melville wrote *Moby Dick*—the first book I read to you when you came into our lives—you wandered with your mother among a collection of delicate, extraordinary fairy houses, searching for inhabitants. At Halloween, you were Tinker Bell.

From the time you first opened your big brown eyes, we had two options. Nothing—or everything. There was really no question.

All the tradition.

Every opportunity to become saturated with culture and ritual.

Hundreds, thousands of moments brimming with genera-tional wealth of experience. All meaning. Every color. Never saying no. Always trying to answer the many, many questions. No one path. Rather, every path.

Because in the end, every single trail should lead to love.

This journey has led to occasional abandonment—cousins you will likely never meet, sadly. And there will come a day, perhaps, when you will look down at the cornucopia of options spread out at your feet, and you will embrace something exclusively, or perhaps nothing at all. Or you will continue to be a child of possibilities, a seeker, never satisfied with any one road, like your mother and father before you.

I hope you will have no fear of the other. And I pray a constant wash of culture and rites and exposure to the potential of the human experience will create empathy. But it will still be a long time before any of that is tested.

For now, you bend toward him, and your grandfather touches your forehead like a conduit, a flesh transfer of his heart and love. It is a moment of pure commitment between you two, unweighted by the politics of worship or institutional dogma.

This is simple. You are his granddaughter. He is your grandfather. But sometimes the simplest sentiment carries the full volume of experience and the memory of a thousand years and a thousand stories.

My little girl, my Durga. Part of me and part of the universe. You hug your grandfather and smile and wait for the next elder to take their place. Your ceremony is just beginning.

OH! SHENANDOAH!

After being cooped up all afternoon hiding from the frigid rain, we decide we've had enough. This is Shenandoah National Park, and even though the (we assume) spectacular views were hidden along Skyline Drive, the moisture shimmered beautifully on the trees and the exhibit on the national park was enlightening.

Still, you need more, and I must admit—so do I. So we say *the heck with it*. Sure, we hadn't brought our heaviest winter clothes with us, but the playground is only a short hike away and getting a little wet and dirty is part of the joy of a national park!

We bundle up in literally every stitch of warm clothes we brought, fling open the door to our tiny, cozy cabin, and march off into the wind.

It's cold. And the rain is coming in sideways. We're at about 2,500 feet here and technically the park is one long ridgeline, so the wind barrels down on us like a freight train. "Daddy, it's really cold!"

"Sure is, baby, you want to turn back?"

But we can see the playground now, and I recognize that look on your face. We aren't turning back.

"No! I want to go down the slide!"

By the time we reach the playground, rain has slithered

down our jackets and into our pants. We're walking in three inches of cold mud. You climb up onto that slide anyway, your hands slipping on the slick wooden steps, and walk across the little bridge, having to brace yourself against the wind. At the top of the slide you look down at me, grim-faced and determined. The slide is like a waterfall.

"Do it," I yell above the maelstrom. "We're wet anyway, it doesn't matter."

You cascade down that thing and splash in the enormous puddle at the foot of the slide like Apollo 11 returning to the Pacific.

You stand up, cold rain dripping off your eyelashes, take a deep breath, and say, "Can we go back to the cabin now? Can you carry me?"

Yes.

* * *

There is no let up. It rains all day and into the evening. There is no view. There is no sun. But something else begins to happen. At a small cafe, tucked into the nearby visitor center, we settle in for a dinner of grilled cheese, fish and chips, and salad. Your mom orders a lovely mommy drink, and I sip a perfectly chilled iced tea. The cafe gets busy. I watch people walk in out of that cold, stomp their feet, and look around, and I can see the stress slip off their shoulders. A couple kids come in. Then an older couple with a tiny, shaggy puppy sit down at the table next to us.

Your eyes grow wide, and your feet begin to shimmy.

"Yes," I say, "but be polite."

You slip down off the chair and tap the older gentleman on the elbow. "May I pet your dog?"

And so there we are, warm, surrounded by travelers from around the world sharing salty French fries. By the time the bluegrass duo starts up, you are best friends with that dog and that couple, and you have eaten nearly an entire, ridiculous slice of something called Mile-High Strawberry Ice Cream Pie.

Outside, the wind howls, but suddenly the banjo makes us forget what's happening beyond the dark, wet glass. You find a tiny space between tables and stomp your feet and clap, and I come join you and get down on my knees to twirl you to the harmony.

The mighty valley gives us that one evening, and you become the Shenandoah's daughter, a daughter of the stars, twirling there high on a ridge, full of sugar and stubborn joy, happy to be on the road even if we can't see the sun. In the morning, we'll be on the run from the angry sea, but tonight we own the valley.

HARD CHOICES

"Daddy, who's that?"

We are standing under the 54th Pennsylvania Monument just off Route 11 along the rolling, gorgeous farmland of the Shenandoah Valley. This small statue with its familiar pose of a Union soldier is one of a few monuments commemorating a northern regiment in Virginia. This isn't a national park. You won't hear about the Battle of New Castle in the schoolbooks. But men died here, blood seeping into the soil under our feet, on the very ground where you sit now, picking dandelions.

"That's a soldier, baby. There was a fight here, a long time ago. That statue marks the spot."

"Who fought? Bad men? Monsters?"

"Yeah, bad men," I say. "But the good men won."

This satisfies your curiosity for now. I want to tell you that the good men haven't won yet. Not really. That we've been fighting for a long, long time. That at some point, you'll have to fight too. That maybe the good men will never win.

"Daddy, look at the flowers and the tiny rocks!" Here we are among the lost towns of the Civil War, my innocent girl gently stacking pebbles along the base of the granite marker. It is so beautiful here—the mountains to the east, the river and fertile valley to the west.

We are here not by design, but rather by necessity. Last

night, as you slept, your mother and I watched news of Hurricane Florence unfold, and we saw the lines of cars full of evacuees heading north—heading this way. We made the difficult decision to abandon our plans for the Carolina coasts. Instead, this morning, we headed west, off the Shenandoah ridge, down into the valley. We had no plans now. Instead, we'd try our luck in West Virginia and Maryland and Western Pennsylvania.

And here in New Castle, where we can smell the wet hay and the wildflowers, where Cow Bane and Iron Weed grow taller than you.

I'm naturally inclined, baby, to regard your good nature and love of the outdoors in juxtaposition to this place of commemorated death, but somehow that feels too easy—this isn't Gettysburg or Antietam. This is some farmer's backyard along a state route. War with a small "w," if that can be a thing, just a footnote in a town that is a footnote itself. And despite all the divides of the past couple years, I love it here—how it smells, how as the traveler approaches the jagged southeast corner of West Virginia, the roads swing down into the sycamores. I love the Waffle House where the waitresses call you darlin' and it takes forever for someone to give you directions. And I love the brick and steel of southern Pennsylvania and Harper's Ferry where the Shenandoah River splits off from the Potomac and you can stand up on the Maryland Heights and look down at the place where a wild man from New York named John Brown made his last stand and foolishly believed others would stand with him.

I know I'm not supposed to, baby, I know. My father, a

World War II vet, would just shake his head whenever I thanked him for his service. He'd say the best way to honor veterans is to not create more veterans. I don't know what he'd think of the sight of you running your finger over the cool granite lettering of this monument. Would he approve of the fistfuls of dirt in your hands? I don't know, but baby, if we can't see the sea this time around, we'll celebrate the soil instead.

WATER

We're startled to learn that children aren't allowed inside Falling Water, Frank Lloyd Wright's masterpiece near Union-town, Pennsylvania. I imagine you'd appreciate the smooth rock floors, the enormous built-in kettle, and the slim stone staircases. The colors, rose and orange, would appeal to everything about you.

I adore this place. I love Wright's sensibility, his stubbornness, how relentlessly specific he was; in a contest between nature and design, nature won every time.

But to not allow you to see it, even in my arms, feels like a betrayal. I sigh. Your mother heads off on a tour, and you and I set off to find what they call the Children's House, the island for misfit kids not allowed to have Falling Water's shadow touch them.

But I won't have it, baby.

"Hey," I say as we head down the lovely walk into the valley where the kid house waits, "want to go see the house anyway?"

You stop to contemplate what I'm asking. I deeply appreciate this about you, this ability to reflect. Even as a baby, it seemed like I could see you thinking.

"Where Mommy is?"

I nod.

"But the man said we had to go to the playhouse."

"We will. After. First we'll go see the other house."

We skirt the playhouse, cut over a wide, muddy lawn, and reconnect with the crushed gravel trail closer to the house and the water, away from any tour groups.

"Water, Daddy, listen!"

It's been decades since I was here last, but I remember that sound. There are a few people down here, but no kids. Everyone is behaving, I guess. We don't care. One tour group is in the house and another is behind us someplace so the little bridge that leads to the front door is wide open.

"What is this, Daddy?" you ask. You stand wide-eyed, my tiny miracle in a ponytail, in front of a singular, sprawling testament to what humans can accomplish. The morning is warm, the sound of the falls under the house roars.

"This is the house, baby, built by a famous architect. It's built right on top of a waterfall."

I lift you up so you can see the water, and we edge a little closer. No one has stopped us yet, but a tour group and a couple docents are approaching.

"Want to go in?" I whisper.

But you surprise me. "No, Daddy, we should go play at the playhouse." You smile and kiss my cheek over and over again and laugh, like you know better. And you do. So we run all the way back, giggling and slipping on the wet grass until the sound of the water has retreated and we're both out of breath.

Later, as we wait for your mother to join us, you pull a handful of tiny stones out of your pocket and hold them in your palm for me to see. Your own architecture. Your own memory of a place you weren't allowed. We'll take them home and build another house with them, content in the memory of the sound of falling water.

WANTED: HEROES

We are settled in for our ride across Southern Pennsylvania, fresh off a visit to Falling Water, cooler packed with treats, the long glorious highway stretching out before us.

From the back seat your mother says, "Isn't Shanksville in Pennsylvania?"

"The place where the plane went down on 9/11? I think so, why?"

She's quiet for a moment, focusing on her phone.

"Oh my gosh!" I say. "Today is the anniversary!"

"Get off at the next exit!" she yells.

None of this was planned, baby. Certainly not the Flight 93 National Memorial on the seventeenth anniversary of the event. But we'd been following our guts these last few days and, oh, the things we'd seen. How were we to know the role you would somehow, incredibly, play in the lives of so many people today? But you would, and it would all begin in a Goodwill store in the middle of nowhere.

* * *

By the time we arrive, it's mid-afternoon and the park is packed. We missed the president and the anniversary ceremony by only a couple hours. The bleachers are still set up and dozens of tour buses and RVs are buzzing around the site.

As we pull up, we watch in wonder as a pickup truck, decorated from top to bottom with flags, Statues of Liberty, and World Trade Center models slowly drives by. Thousands of bubbles float out from the truck bed, shimmering in the cloudy sky. There are vets on motorcycles hugging and shaking hands. Tour buses from all over the country idle, tour groups of folks in wheelchairs, on crutches, and hunched over walkers mill around. Families push strollers.

To you, we are just going to a park. On the way here, I tried to explain this will be a special park, a place to think about things and remember people. But I'm not ready to talk to you about 9/11. So I don't really know how this will go.

As I'm unbuckling you and we're getting ready to walk the long path to the memorial, you say, "Daddy, I want to wear the costume!"

"Here?"

"Please, yes, please!"

At a stop off the highway, we took a bathroom break at a Goodwill store. You found a bright red mask and cape and we took it with us for the coming Halloween.

"Please let me wear it!" you moan.

I'm out of my league here. What are we doing? There are TV cameras and vets in leather jackets on Harleys. Would that be . . . I don't know, disrespectful?

"Let her wear it." Your mother touches my elbow and smiles, always the voice of reason. The brave one. "It'll be okay."

I fasten the Velcro cape around your shoulders and slide the red mask over your eyes.

"Like the Incredibles, Daddy!"

I set you on the pavement and take a deep breath. Your mother and I take a hand on either side of you and we begin to walk.

* * *

The site sits on a couple thousand acres of farmland, and the memorial itself is enormous and subdued at the same time; there's a long runway-like walkway leading to a small orientation visitor center, then a larger museum, then the wall of names and finally a lookout platform rising above a hillock that overlooks the actual crash site. The memorial is designed in the direction of the flight plan that the doomed airliner came in.

The National Parks Service took great pains to not sensationalize the site, to veer purposefully away from nationalism and focus on the heroic acts of sacrifice of the passengers that fateful day. It is a beautiful, respectful tribute.

You don't know any of this, little one. You know we are outside. And it's one of the first warm days we've had on this road trip. You know there is space to move, things to touch and flowers everywhere. And as we walk, you become aware that people are beginning to notice.

A docent near a large map of the park smiles and says, "Oh, honey, you're so pretty!" A vet with a round belly and black vest filled with patches and medals smiles and gives me the thumbs up. I smile back—I don't know what else to do. Couples point at you. Some folks whisper. I'm shocked when one lady, as we pass on the long walkway up to the memorial, says, "Thank you."

Near the viewing platform, a tall, dark-haired park ranger watches you approach.

"Is that a policeman, Daddy?" you ask.

"No, baby, he's called a park ranger."

"What does he do?"

"Let's ask him," I say.

I lift you up, but even in my arms, the ranger still has a few inches on us. His name is David. I whisper in your ear, "Ask him."

"Mr. David, what do you do?"

"Well, sometimes people have questions, other times they just want to talk," he says. "I try to help people."

"Like a superhero?" you ask.

Park Ranger David takes off his sunglasses and hat and bends toward you, only inches from your face. There is no one here, no audience. This isn't a performance. He is talking only to you.

"What's your name?" he asks.

"Uma."

"Well, Uma, this place was built to remember heroes. But today, you're the only superhero here."

His eyes well up, as do mine. I hope you remember that moment, baby.

"I'm an Incredible," you tell him.

"You sure are," he says.

We part ways, and I put you down. There are only a few people at the lookout, but when they see you coming, they move off as though they are making room for you, clearing that space to allow you a moment's meditation. And you do.

You walk right up to the edge and pause. Like you're reading the words.

Like you're a nearly four-year-old who somehow understands.

* * *

After, we visit the exhibit and your mother listens to some of the recordings. I can't, I don't want to cry. We check out the gift shop and you pick out a fridge magnet. We drive over to a sculpture called the Tower of Voices, a half-built memorial with forty wind chimes to commemorate the passengers. You call it a singing tower. We meet a couple from a nearby town who have a granddaughter like you. On our way back, you pluck a daisy off the sidewalk and hold it tightly in the car, and as you fall asleep, the flower remains locked in your fist.

We're quiet as we drive away, heading east toward home, the day slowly seeping into night. Grateful for the road. Grateful for each other. And grateful for the sleeping superhero we call our daughter.

SNOW IS FLEETING

There's this terrible meme going around about finding joy in snow—something like: if you don't find joy in snow, then you will have less joy in your life, but you'll have the same amount of snow. I've enjoyed teasing my snow-hating friends with it, but really, baby, that sentiment is sort of silly.

The construct of the faux philosophy assumes that you should be happy about things that are out of your control—if you can't do anything about it, then you may as well enjoy it. But replace the word snow with anything else, and the idea falls apart. If you don't find joy in the plane falling on your house, then you will have less joy in your life, but you'll still have the same amount of wreckage on your house. See?

But I digress. I actually love winter. I get a little exercise, the trees look nice, and I'll likely go sledding up to when—and most likely while—I'm using a walker as a sled.

Mostly, though, like any other authentic connection to the natural world, it isn't the grand gestures that create awe. I'm often less impressed by a glacier then I am by how quiet my neighborhood sounds on the evening of a gentle snowfall as the three of us walk hand in hand down the middle of the empty street, our lungs clear and clean, and you look up at me with the fire of wonder in your eyes and a few flakes get caught up on your eyelashes and you are suddenly crystalline, a tiny Skadi, the embodiment of winter.

On this afternoon, the day after a storm, I come home from work to find you fully engaged in the first snowperson of the year, and you are glowing.

Writer and psychoanalyst Mary Lamia talks about the emotional memory of a repeating event like snowfall—in particular the first snowfall of any given season, which she calls a cued recall. In other words, because those early days of snow left such vivid and powerful impressions on our young minds, every time it snows again, our minds are programmed to remember and bring the emotion front and center.

For me, because I loved snow, and my parents did too, the emotional recall is always positive. Add to that, baby, that you are now building a landscape—a whole mind city from scratch—of emotional recall, and the first snowfall becomes even more intense, even more lovely for us both.

But how fleeting is this snow? How tied to cycles and shades of birth and death and rebirth. One of my favorite photos is of your grandmother when she was thirteen in the snow-covered backyard of your great-grandmother's home; she's standing on a runner sled, holding the reins, grinning, expecting a push or pull or maybe just a cold gust to sweep her into the air. Or another picture of your aunt and myself, buried in snow, snowballs in hand—her in a pink snowsuit, me in a brown one—laughing with frozen cheeks. And now you, your third winter, nearly as tall as your creation, a black-haired Elsa and her mohawked Olaf.

The snow will fall, the geography will transform, the ice will rage, and then, as always, the crocuses will signal renewal. The seasons are as fleeting as life itself, as time, as *our* time. The memories, weighted with emotion like tree branches bending under wet snow, will form and fall away and come back again at the next first snowfall. And you'll be there, and I'll be with you for as long as I can, and someone will eventually replace me, the cycle will continue and the snow will always find its way.

THREE LITTLE DEATHS

Does "daddy" count as my name? I'll choose to believe so.

We find the monarch butterfly near death in the middle of a wide pedestrian mall. The poor creature is shivering, jerking its wings for the final few times.

"Daddy, the butterfly is hurt!" You don't even hesitate. You bend down and gently pluck him from the pavement, letting him rest in your palm, a wide-eyed three-year-old and a dying insect. "Can you help him?"

Mexican tradition offers some waymarks when navigating the stages of death. Generally, there are three: the moment you realize you are mortal and will die, the moment you do actually die, and the final time someone remembers your name.

The day is coming, little one, when that first death will be upon us and our conversation will exist in the realm of your first real existential pain, and you'll understand not just that we die but what that actually means. We're not there yet, but we're close. I dread the day.

For today, however, I get to eye level with you and explain that this little fellow has likely led a good life, has filled people's hearts with happy colors and the beauty of his fluttering, but now the time has come when he will die. "We can't help him, baby," I say.

And there's a pause, an aching moment where you consider

this truism and you watch, stock still, this delicate creature in your hand take its last breaths. Suddenly, I feel like maybe we've crossed a line, like we just left behind the little girl I knew and are starting from scratch now, different, slightly colder.

But you reach out a finger and run it along the outside of his wing and move your little face just inches from your palm. "Poor baby," you say. "Daddy, can I put him by a flower? He'll like it there."

I nod. And I scramble to think of all those I loved, all those who have died twice, whom I can prevent from final death. I think their names. I write them. Ceil. Joseph. Fred. Florence. Teddy. Mary. Viola. Fritz. Joey. Alan. Annette. Sara. Nabil. Cindy.

God, the list is long.

The two of us stand there for a few seconds, watching the butterfly. You've tucked him into a planter, near some flowers, on a soft bed of bark mulch. Momentarily, he'll die there. And the last experience that fragile creature will have had in his short time on earth will be that of the compassion of a three-year-old girl with big round eyes and warm hands.

And I think again, does "daddy" count as my name? How long will you remember me? How long will I live?

A SPLENDID FISH

This morning, we were late for school. You had some bad dreams. I'm nursing the beginnings of a cold. I can't find my gloves. You know how it is.

I'm hustling you out of the house, about as close to actually pushing you out the door as I dare, when you very deliberately stop me, putting your palm up like a crossing guard stopping traffic, and say, "Daddy, wait, I have to show you something!"

The inside glass door is covered with a thin layer of condensation. You step up, nose nearly to the glass and begin to draw: first, a somewhat wobbly circle. Then three of four lines coming out of the top of the circle. One eye, a second. And then a wide smile.

"It's you, Daddy! See!"

Why do you crush me like this, child? So often, so unexpectedly. Do you really have this gentle a soul, or are you the most devious child on the planet, knowing exactly the sort of action that will stop me in my tracks and melt me?

I've lost track of the number of times I've asked this question of myself, but today, for the first time, I put it to you after we've settled ourselves in the car for the ride to school.

"Uma, I have a question for you."

"What, Daddy?"

"What is art?"

You don't pause. "A turkey feather!" In class this week, you've been doing craft projects of coloring turkey feathers.

"Okay, yes, but I mean that little drawing you made of me on the window, is that art?"

"Nooooooo! That was a window!"

"What if you took a crayon and made that picture of me on a paper, would that be art?"

"Nooooooo! That's you!"

"What about that building? Is that art?"

"That's a building!"

"What about the song on the radio, is that art?"

"That's the Cure!"

"No, no, that's Neil Young, baby!" And the moment passes as I spend the rest of the ride lecturing you on the difference between *Harvest Moon* and *Disintegration*.

You're not ready quite yet to consider the meaning of art, but you're getting there. You know that I write for a living. You know I talk in front of people. You want to come with me. But you're not ready to call it art. But yet, you get better every day. We have this game where you draw some crazy abstract scribble and I turn it into a recognizable picture, a dinosaur or spaceship. I have whole notebooks full of that. And when you really bear down and say you're drawing a fish, you're at that stage where it really does look like a fish!

But art? Well . . .

The conductor Frank Albinder wrote that "Art is work . . . And that's not a bad thing. By bringing music into the lives of others, we can provide inspiration, comfort, delight, and peace. It's not a bad way to make a living!"

Meanwhile, Oscar Wilde thought art was the manifestation of individualism, while Thomas Merton felt art was a means by which we can record our own truth. Frank Lloyd Wright felt art was the echo of nature. And Tolstoy, well, art was everything. To him, it was "indispensable for the life and progress toward the well-being of individuals and of humanity."

But what is art to a four-year-old? Isn't an artist that has no concept or opinion of art the purest artist of them all? To you, baby, it's not work. It's not difficult. You have no models or competition. You are fine using any medium—glass, paper, backs of bills. Your stick man, your cat, your scrawl is utterly authentic, untainted by the concern of the audience, social media, or what or whether anyone cares.

Why are there no museums dedicated to toddlers? Why do collectors not pay millions for a splendid fish—crayon on notebook.

Today, I have no answer. You'll have to find your own way, baby, and I suppose that's what art is anyway. Just a tiny pink finger on a pane of wet glass, and the warm air that will eventually make the art just a memory.

WE GIVE THANKS

"Daddy, did you know that Thanksgiving is because of the Maryflower?"

I look up, startled. "The—do you mean the Mayflower, how do you—?"

"They came to Pimith Rock."

You have my full attention. "Well, actually, the Pilgrims first landed in Provincetown, baby—"

"No, Daddy! Pimith Rock!"

"Okay, okay, jeez, fine, for now."

"It's a rock."

"Yes."

There's a long pause. We look at each other.

I say, "We can visit Plymouth, uh, I mean *Pimith* Rock sometime if you'd like."

You nod. "I can be an Indian."

"What?"

"I can wear my Indian feathers when we go to Pimith Rock."

"Your—what, wait, feathers? Oh no, I don't think—"

"There were Indians, daddy!"

"Yes, I know!" I realize I'm arguing with a three-year-old.

I also realize that you are getting so far ahead of me, suddenly, every day, that I may never catch up. Honestly, I had no expectation of having to tiptoe over the Thanksgiving story minefield with you for some time yet, but apparently your teachers have other ideas and you are like a fact sponge.

So here we are.

Here's the thing about gratitude or thankfulness. I want that to be an everyday part of your life experience. I want you to not just understand what it means to have more than so many others, but I want that thankfulness to exist in your heart every day, and I want that gratitude to extend outward. It's not enough to be thankful for what you have; the next step is to give to those who don't.

For now, family will be enough. You've already offered to help your momma and your aunt prepare dinner. You've already said you want to watch football with your cousins. This is a good start.

Forget the Pilgrims and the rock and the Indians, for now. Let's just begin there. We'll have time for that later. But I do have a couple full days now to offer some . . . alternatives to your teachers, for when you return to school.

I lean in close, like I'm telling you a secret. "Did you know, baby, that nine other countries celebrate Thanksgiving?"

"Do they have pilgrims?"

"Nope. But tell your teachers that in South Korea, they wrestle! And in China, they eat Moon Cake!"

Your eyes are wide as saucers. "Cake? For Thanksgiving?"

And so it begins . . .

JUST FIFTEEN MINUTES

I have a vague memory, a wobbly, fuzzy story, told to me by my grandfather (or perhaps my aunt, or maybe even my dad, or possibly I created it in a dream) of a newly married butcher at Buffalo's Broadway Market around the turn of the twentieth century wheeling his bride down the meat aisle in a wheelbarrow to the applause of other meatmen. Those brothers in meat would toss chunks of prime cuts and cheese into the wheelbarrow, valuable wedding gifts at the time.

There is a less vague memory of my grandmother's two brothers owning a butcher shop there in the 1930s, or perhaps later.

I have deeply ingrained memories, however, of my aunt, her hand holding my shoulder in a vice grip as we walked through the market, elbow to elbow with men in bright blue Sunday jackets and little old ladies in babushkas. And of a long Formica counter with spinning seats, a great metal grill, and of women with hair that smelled like vanilla who called me hon and held steaming glass pots of burned coffee. My aunt would order three pierogi, cheese, my favorite, with butter and onions. I'd eat one, she two. And the great whirlwind of that marketplace, the center of everything Polish in Buffalo, would spin around us.

Today, Santa was arriving at the market, and it was a rare

opportunity for me to take you, baby, to a place that played a keystone role in my childhood, a place of sausage and sponge candy, of glass ornaments and painted eggs.

You, your mom, and I are greeted near the elevator by several hideous sculptures of children fashioned entirely out of used tires, and it's at that moment I realize that was then, this is now.

You step out into the main aisle and ask, "Is this a fair, Daddy, what do you do here?"

A long time has passed since this market in my hometown was the center of Polish commerce and culture, and if you look closely—squint at just the proper angle behind the flea market booths selling candy cane socks and the chili powder dealers—the bones of this nearly 130-year-old institution are faint, but still there. The back wall still contains a row of meat and fish dealers, their fresh product on ice, selling turkey gizzards and whitefish, strings of polish sausage still hanging here and there. The horseradish man is still there, and the woman selling caramelized cashews. And the familiar cement floor and the sound of footsteps clunking over the metal drains still echoes.

But the cover band wailing away Neil Young and Grateful Dead tunes seems out of sorts, though you do a little shuffle as we pass and that perks up the scraggly group of cold shoppers at the iron tables, all waiting, one suspects, for the next bus to pass by outside.

And despite the dreary surroundings, you make out like a bandit, but then you always do. One woman hands you a whole bag of chocolates in the shape of Buffaloes. Another gives you jelly beans. One man gives you a stuffed Santa for free because, he claims, he was just trying to get rid of it anyway. You promptly rename Santa—Pumpkin.

I try to find the bits and pieces of what this place meant to me and condense that into some tangible experience for you to hold on to. We turn a corner and I find a familiar vendor, my long lunch counter, the one my aunt took me to all those years ago. There's been several different owners since then, of course, and the prices are higher, but it looks the same, smells the same.

We sit on the spinning stools, and a lady in a blue apron comes over. I'm thrilled when she gets down eye level with you and says, "Hiya, hon!"

I order us a cheese pierogi, and you and I sit and sip orange juice and coffee until it arrives. This is exactly as I remember it, the smells of onion and butter, the coffee tasting deliciously old, but perfectly boiled. I delicately slice a piece of the pierogi for you, mop up a bit of butter, and carefully feed it to you.

"Uuuuuugh, Daddy!" You wrinkle your nose. "I don't like it. Can we go home now?"

Your mother just shrugs, but she understands me. Maybe she's the only one who does. "I'm going to take her to the bathroom, and we'll meet you back at the elevators in fifteen minutes?"

I nod, she pats my shoulder, and you two leave me at the counter alone.

I take a deep breath and slice off another, larger piece, only this time add a huge dollop of sweet cheese and close my eyes as I shovel the fork full into my mouth.

It tastes like memories.

And I realize suddenly that this moment must just be mine, can be mine alone. That as much as I look for every opportunity to bridge that gap between us, to connect between time and space, sometimes, that's not possible.

I have fifteen minutes, your mother said. That should be enough. And with every bite, every jolt of salt and dough, washed down by bitter hot coffee, the sounds of the meat cutters and the Christmas bells and the clap of a heel on concrete, I begin to feel my aunt's hand on my shoulder calling me back.

Today, baby, I'm going back without you. But just today. Just fifteen minutes. Just one perfectly fried cheese pierogi until the waitress scoops up my plate. I run my fingers over the Formica worn smooth from decades of fingertips, gulp down the last swig from my Styrofoam cup, and I leave to find you again.

"How was it," your mother asks.

"Good," I say, "really good."

MY STARDUST MELODY

The other day, your mother and I were talking about something that happened years before you were born, and you asked why we didn't take you along.

"That was way before you were here, baby," your mother said.

"Before I was in your tummy?"

"Before that," I said. "You were just stardust up there in the universe, just waiting for somebody to bring you home."

Surprisingly, you didn't ask me what the heck I was talking about. Being stardust seemed reasonable.

Astrophysicist Neil deGrasse Tyson spills a lot of ink talking about the connectivity of our own atoms to the universe, how we are not figuratively—but literally—stardust. "It's not that we are better than the universe, we are part of the universe," he writes. "We are in the universe and the universe is in us."

How reassuring, then, to *be of* and to *be unique* at once. To be a daughter of the cosmos and to be our own specific universal bundle at the same time.

To have you—and for you to have us—as the briefest of flashes against the backdrop of the endless darkness—and then to return to the darkness. Each of us our own pinprick flash of light, like millions of light bulbs exploding every moment. Individually, providing barely enough light to matter, but as a whole, lighting up the world.

As a boy, I never set my sights on being an astronaut, or part of NASA, though I was deeply interested in space in the way that most children are drawn to the mysterious and the unknown. I loved science fiction and movies about spaceships and exploration. I loved reading about robots—memorized Asimov's Three Rules of Robotics, felt drawn to the concept of created life, felt sorry for Frankenstein's monster and the Runaway Robot alike.

I remember a moment in my parent's car coming home at night from a family visit, watching the moon out my window and asking, "Daddy, why is the moon following us?"

He just laughed, as unable to answer the question then as I am now. But I never actually wished to leave the Earth. Do you, baby? Over the last few months, we've seemed to breach the subject of infinity over and over. Why is it sometimes cold and sunny at once? Can we go to Jupiter? Why is Earth called Earth? How far to the moon? Mostly, I don't know the answers; we'll learn them together. Sometimes, I get the feeling that you're more interested in the questions than in the answers.

There are real answers to all these questions, grounded in astronomy and physics, but how miraculous is it, my stardust child, that you are even here to begin with, asking them.

year five
WOOD

PAPER DOLLS

After a long weekend with your mother away on a business trip, you and I settle in for our final evening on our own. Tonight, a surprise, or perhaps an experiment in paper.

You're unsure at first as I spread out the papers, tape, scissors, string and figures on the table.

"What do we do?" you ask.

"We cut out costumes and dress them," I proclaim, acting as if this was the most natural thing to me, like I've played with paper dolls a million times. I never have.

But nothing is really new. The Japanese were folding paper into figures as far back as 800 AD, and the Balinese since before the Common Era. There's a paper doll card in the German National Museum that dates around 1650, and "Little Fanny" was produced for British kids in 1810.

And here we are with Molly and Samantha doing the same; the same tabs, the same process, the same evening before bedtime, the same dim light in a house that's a home.

"I can cut them?" you ask.

"Of course!"

We sort the costumes, read the little descriptions out loud. And you cut. And cut. And the paper swirls there under the kitchen lights like confetti, and paper toes get chopped off and tabs go missing and Molly's arm needs a fair amount of tape to patch her up.

We do this for two straight hours. When I see you beginning to slow, and your eyes droop, it's you who finally decides, "Daddy, I think I'm done with this."

"Shall we keep all this?" I ask.

"No, we can throw it out," you say, then after a pause, "Daddy, I think I like dolls that can stand up a little more."

"I understand kid-o."

But as we're sweeping the evening of papers into the trash, you stop me. "Well, maybe Samantha and Molly can go on my wall, though."

We keep the two paper dolls, and you help me clip them to your display wall—two little girls in old-timey clothes bridging the gap between you and generations of little girls before you. The beat goes on.

10,000 DAYS LEFT

Yesterday, near midnight, I wrote a note to you to place under your pillow. The note begins: "My Dearest Uma, thank you so much for the beautiful tooth . . ."

But as I was writing, I was thinking, how many teeth do you have, how many more evenings like this will there be? So I did some math.

I have about 10,000 days left assuming I reach the American average of eighty years old. That's it, baby. Subtract the time sleeping, or the time I'm at work, or the times you'll be, well, wherever you'll be, and . . . it's best to not do *that* math.

And if it is indeed our tenuous grip to this mortal coil that gives us strength and incentive in this life, well, I'm grateful for your help in forcing me to step up my game.

Besides, as I sat there writing this note as the Tooth Fairy, it occurred to me that this is sort of nice. I mean, there's really no industrial consumer machine surrounding this little ritual, is there? Sure, there's a couple movies and some fancy toothbrushes, but really, we're on our own here—just your parents sprinkling glitter on a couple bucks to slip under your pillow in the hope that you stay a little girl for a while longer. You, our stardust mortality clock, so close now to breaking free of the myths that tether you to wonder.

In the morning, you leap out of bed, clutching the Tooth Fairy's gift. You say, "Look, Daddy, look!"

And as I'm reading the note I wrote to you, you're grinning, and there it is: that adult tooth is coming right in behind the one you just lost. This feels like time is in a hurry. I think, how many teeth do you have left, baby, and how many days do we have?

IMPERFECT LENS

Can I be present in a moment and document it at the same time? Is that moment of esthetic revelation—that split second when an image or landscape or child moves you to reach for your camera—even a real epiphany?

After all, the first time I laid eyes on the Grand Canyon, I cried. No photo exists of that soul movement. Sitting in a rocking chair with you, baby, that first time, a defining turning point, the instant of my shedding the trappings of my old life and becoming a dad—no picture of that.

Being present must exist only in the slipstream of time and absent of anything but awe. Capturing that awe seems like cheating time.

Or does it? The photographer Danielle Hark talks about photography as being able to capture the outside world with the light of your inner world. In other words, the more tuned in to your inside—who you are, your place in the cosmos, your inner eye—then the more stories your photos can convey.

"If you're sad, you don't need to photograph someone crying to convey that emotion or story," she writes. "You just need to view the world as *you*. A macro photo of a single drop of dew can convey a narrative of agonizing sadness, or delight and joy, if you let it."

If you let it.

Look what that school photographer "let" in. For the fourth year in a row, baby, you've owned that cheap stool in front of that bland, dark green sheet. You've walked straight up and claimed that moment.

I wonder—does a pre-school photographer set out to capture the moment, do they seek awe? Do they cry when they get home, not from exhaustion but from the day-long torrent of conducting children's emotions, from those who wail to those who frown, to those, like you, who beam like the sun.

What a job, to try to make every three-year-old smile—or to capture the authenticity of a frown.

Well, if style is about the mechanics of a photo and aesthetics is about how the photo makes the viewer feel, then that certainly explains all three angles of your annual sitting: the photographer's noise-free, grounded setting, your explosion of charm, and my melancholy of seeing how lovely and how adult you are becoming. Style. Subject. Reaction. Really, the recipe for art, generally.

I recall a particular episode—perhaps third or fourth grade—of my own series of annual walks to the gym photographer. I'm wearing a light blue zipper cardigan with white lines and a dark brown wide-collared shirt. My teeth are half missing, and I have a cowlick that sticks straight up from the top of my head. The background was a farm scene (how puzzling is that?) and we leaned casually on a plastic fence. I folded my hands together at the top post. What a mess it all was.

The aesthetics of such a combination are so deeply buried, it's a wonder the picture makes me feel anything but confused.

Not ashamed though, baby, because imperfection, it seems to me, goes hand in hand with mindfulness.

Jonathan Foust, a world-renowned meditation instructor and freelance photographer, talks a lot about what he calls "finding the middle," that fine line between experiencing awe and actually taking a picture of it. Capturing awe *and* experiencing it at the same time. And that moment, more often than not, arrives at the moment the photographer, and the photographer's subject, stops striving for perfection.

In fact, Foust says, "taking pictures is a sort of perpetual training in the art of imperfection."

By that standard, we have arrived at perfection. And I know it's perfection, because your hair is a bit jangled and your hair bands are different colors and maybe you should have worn a brighter color—but all that imperfection makes you, you. I know your hair is mussed because you played hard in gym, and you picked those barrettes. And you don't care. And I don't care. And that photographer likely didn't even have to ask you to smile, because somehow that's just your vibe.

The light shines on you, and you shine right back. The moment is by design and by accident, a trifle and steeped with meaning. And in the end, you move on, another child takes your seat and the imperfect you—now a fridge magnet—lives on, another chapter in your yearly, impossible, impermanent moment of grace.

GIVE 'EM THE CANDY

Today is candy day, baby. Well, technically it was at night last week, but the city got spooked by a lousy weather report of rain that never happened and . . . here we are. Sunday afternoon.

But you know what, who cares? The streets of our neighborhood are surging with kids, teens, and a lot of adults. The weather is mild, the traffic light, and we find ourselves walking right in the middle of the street at times. You are holding hands with your little friend Oscar, each of you leaning into your heavy candy bags.

There's a lot happening here today, but let me start with a proclamation—today, on this day, when the veil between the living and the dead is the thinnest, when the bonfires are lit to ward off spirits, when the shadow of Samhain drifts over our modern streets, there's only one rule—give 'em candy.

A little kid wants two Smarties and not one? Let them have it. A teenager wearing a Freddie mask is desperately holding on to a sliver of childhood? Candy for them! Bedraggled parents with sore feet looking for a Milky Way sugar rush to get them through the night? Here's a full-sized bar for you!

How beautiful then—traditions aside—to have a day when you can knock on a stranger's door and be given a sweet. How human, and lovely, and funny. This night isn't about growing up or not. It's about making people happy. And if someone can be made happy with a Tootsie Roll, give them out in handfuls.

(As an aside, the same goes for other holidays. Why complain if someone puts their Christmas tree up on the day after Halloween? Why complain if they leave their lights up all year long? Let people be happy!)

Meanwhile, you work the candy trade like a champ. You wore your Super Girl outfit to the school party to great effect—the only girl super in a wave of princesses. But today, at the last moment, you decided to slip into your dino wrangler outfit, a gift from your aunt. A wise choice, baby. The outfit is warmer than Super Girl and ratcheted the adorable level to eleven.

No ghost, witch, or ghoul is impervious to your charm. Near a beaten-down fence, a guy dressed like Michael Myers bends over and lets you take a picture with him. Near a front porch covered with pumpkins, a fog machine growls awake, and you float through that mist like you have high beams.

And up high on a porch, a witch sits surrounded by spiders. When you approach, she cackles and says, "No one gets my candy without telling me a joke!"

You don't even hesitate. "Why did the chicken cross the road?"

"Hmmmm," says the witch, "why?"

"To get to the other side!" You scream the answer like a spell, triumphantly. I'm terribly proud. You get a handful of candy for remembering one of the oldest jokes in modern times. Did you know, baby, that that joke has been dated back to an issue of New York City's *Knickerbocker Magazine* from

1847? You told a joke from the same year *Wuthering Heights* was published and Thomas Edison was born.

At the same time that you are drifting in the wake of a nineteenth-century anti-joke, you are also carrying on in the realm of the existential. The modern culture philosopher who goes by the curious name Epicurus of Albion writes that Halloween allows for the most direct example of adopting an identity that one is not.

You are no longer a little girl, but rather Super Girl and everyone identifies you as such, and in return you express the characteristics of your new identity. You are no longer a little girl inside a dinosaur costume, but rather you are literally riding a dinosaur.

"On Halloween, the social norm grants them to have the freedom to be something other than their ordinary selves," Epicurus writes. "Clothing their person as a fictional character offers them the freedom to forget themselves, a break from vocations, respite from anxieties and even freedom away from their own names!"

Tomorrow, sadly, were you to go to school in a Batman costume, society would suspect there was something wrong. How depressing. But I digress.

The day marches on—the same day that we have set our clocks back, so daylight is fleeting. Even by mid-afternoon, the first hints of evening start to creep in and the kids slow down. You eat a Milk Dud for the first time. We discover a house giving away full-sized Snickers bars—like hitting the lottery. And finally, as the day wanes, we discover your limitation when a man comes to the door dressed as a frog but wearing a Creature from the Blue Lagoon mask.

"Uh, Daddy, do you want to see him closer?" you ask. So we go up to that door together.

Before long, you're ready to head home; even a dinosaur's feet get tired eventually. How many of these days do you and I have left, baby. Six? Eight? Not many. You and I walk hand in hand back to our home, back to our routine, back to who we really are—one more day closer to the spirits.

But as we approach the door, you notice our next-door neighbor still on her porch, a bucket of treats at the ready. She sees you and smiles. You look at me.

"Go on!" I say. My baby dinosaur, my authentic child, my benevolent spirit.

BREAD IS LIFE

I have no tactile experience with bread, baby. At least not before I married your mother.

When I was a child, my mother used to make me grilled cheese where she'd cut the sandwich into two triangles, invert them and put a pickle spear down the middle to make it look like a butterfly. My dad loved ryes and pumpernickels. But for the life of me, I can't remember a time when anyone in my family actually made a loaf of bread from scratch. Muffins, cupcakes, cookies, sure. But not fresh bread.

That changed somewhat when I married into your mother's family. Your uncle is a baker, a master of yeast and flour. His bread looks like art. Your grandfather and mother make it from scratch. I got your mother a cast iron pot to bake bread in once, and it turned out she already had one. She kept it anyway so she could bake two at a time. I did it myself a couple times, but I don't feel like I have the chops to make it taste like hers.

"All sorrows are less with bread," said Cervantes. Surely, he meant your mother's bread.

You, baby, are of course game for anything. Last week, I came home to discover you and your mother coated in flour as a baking marathon progressed. You are elbow deep in the white stuff—flour being the part of the process you like the most. Your mother has given you your own ball of dough. So I pour myself a cup of coffee and watch you work. You have a little wooden roller and a heart shaped cookie cutter. You roll the dough out over and over, sprinkling flour each time, mash it up into a ball and then roll it out again. You cut out a heart, press it back into the dough ball and cut it out again.

And it occurs to me, watching you, that maybe I do know a little something about bread, though not the kind that goes in the oven. You aren't baking, you are playing, using touch and smell, the joy of companionship and the proximity of loved ones to center your little kid self.

You are being in the moment. You are practicing mindfulness.

Growing up in a Roman Catholic neighborhood, in a Roman Catholic family, such abstract practices like mindfulness really weren't much a part of my day—unless you count being mindful of putting out the candles as an altar boy before leaving the church.

But there was spiritual bread, because there is John 6:35—"I am the bread of life. He who comes to Me shall never hunger, and he who believes in Me shall never thirst."

As a young man, I never gave much thought to the Gospels, preferring the razzmatazz of the Old Testament and its brimstone and fire. That's where my namesake was tossed into a den of lions and where Jonah was swallowed by a whale. Those were stories with action and danger.

It took a long time—after leaving the church, discovering other cultural touchstones, having you—for the concept of the Bread of Life to resonate more strongly. I recall how often, as middle schoolers, we would joke about receiving the sacrament of Eucharist and exactly which part of Jesus we were eating when we did. It was middle school; you can fill in the rest.

Let's not even open the can of worms that is transubstantiation, baby. That's a conversation for another time.

For now, as I watch your little hands roll and flatten, squeeze and tug that tiny ball of dough, it feels like there's something deeper happening.

Let's call it the sustenance of the soul. Yours or mine? I suppose it doesn't matter. Fancy or not, processed and sliced or baked in clay, you are once again following not in a cultural line, but a human one that dates to the dawn of agriculture.

There's evidence that humans—little kids, I like to imagine—in Europe 30,000 years ago were doing something like what you're doing now. Recently, archaeologists in the Black Desert in Jordan uncovered two buildings, 15,000 years old, each containing a large circular stone fireplace within which charred breadcrumbs were found. That wee bit of flour in your hand connects you to our prehistoric ancestors.

After a time, your little bread ball is removed from the oven and your mother places it delicately onto a piece of aluminum foil to cool.

You. Made. That.

"That's your first bread, baby," I say.

You gently place it next to your mother's—magnificent, as usual—loaf and laugh. "It's so small. Can we eat it?"

"Of course!"

I get a knife and gently cut the bread ball into three pieces. The crust is very hard because of the size, but the inside is soft.

And there we stand—in the kitchen of a warm home, in the year 2019, a small family with a small slice of bread, performing a ritual of sustenance and faith that extends far beyond cultural or spiritual boundaries.

"Daddy, the crust is too hard."

"You'll get better at it," I say. "Like your mother."

Or your grandmother. Or whomever was using that fireplace in Jordan. The Divine Transaction complete, the staff of life consumed, your hands and face chalky with white dust, we complete one more circle and the universe inches one step closer to perfection.

WOOD

In the front yard of your grandparents' house, there is a lovely tree stump. Do you remember it, baby? Even in its cutting, your grandparents have plans. The larger pieces are used for the garden. The single tall stump will become a platform for vines and flowers. The roots of that tree will remain long after your grandparents, your parents, and even you are gone.

And so that tree, a giver of life even after death, has become something of an enigma to you—you seem far more interested in it after it was cut then when it grew.

On a recent visit, we play in the yard, and you are drawn, as always, to the tree. Years ago, we attended a summer fair and one of the vendors there, the Society for the Protection of New Hampshire Forests, was handing out thin strips of a cut tree, a sapling really. Each circular crosscut was, perhaps, the size of a half dollar. We kept going back, and back. These cross cuts where you could see the age lines so clearly fascinated you. We still have them.

A neighbor has constructed a tiny fairy house in the cracks and crevasses of a nearby tree, and you never fail to visit. In our own yard, you bring rock and shell offerings to the stone Buddha that rests on one of our own stumps, and in the fall, we go apple picking and you beg me to lift you up into the trees to reach for the reddest fruit.

And it occurs to me that the trees—much more than any other natural elemental—are raising you along with us.

I think of the great German Romantic poet Friedrich Holderlin, who wrote:

I was raised by the song
Of the murmuring grove
And loving I learned
Among flowers.

I adore the idea of the trees speaking. On a hike up to a fire tower not long ago, a heavy wind blew through the tops of the trees and the barks ached and groaned in their song of sway.

"What's that sound, Daddy?" you asked.

"That's the wind blowing the tops of the trees, baby."

We stood and listened to the trees for a long time.

Now we wander over to the big stump cut sharply and perfectly, and you say to me as if discovering this for the first time, "Daddy, do you want to know how old this tree is?"

"Sure," I say, "show me."

And so you count, slowly and deliberately. The air, cool and damp with autumn, your flesh connecting with the newly cut wood—a little girl absorbing the energy that still exists inside the trunk. The process takes a while for you, your little finger inching its way over the yellowing trunk.

"Twenty-seven, Daddy, this tree has twenty-seven rings."

I suspect the number is higher than that, but you're proud of your counting.

"You just did some science there, baby," I say.

"I did?"

"Yup, that's called dendrochronology."

You give me a look.

"Scientists can figure out the weather and what's in the air and what's in the ground based on the rings of a tree."

"What's in this one?" you ask.

"I dunno, you'd have to be a scientist to figure that out."

"I think it's just dirt."

"I think you may be right."

Do you know, baby, that your engagement with that tree— the art and science of ring counting—is over 2,000 years old? It was a Greek botanist way back in BC who first mentioned that tree wood has rings. And none other than Leonardo da Vinci himself that was the first to suggest that trees form rings annually.

My tiny Leonardo . . . my Renaissance toddler.

There are, of course, other ways your path will cross with trees. There will be climbing and, perhaps, tree houses. There will be animals in trees. And at some point, you'll ask me what a certain tree is, and I'll have to answer that, so tree-learning is most certainly on the horizon.

But for now, you seem content to just touch, to pick up leaves and to chase the squirrels. You know that trees are life-givers, you know that's where fruit comes from and falls from and deep down inside, you darn well know that trees hold secrets as well. Fairies come from them, magic happens because of them, and if you listen closely, the trees will talk to you.

Talk back, baby. And teach me how to hear.

RAINBOW FEET

"Come on, Daddy, it's time to explore the city!"

We are foot loose and fancy free on this fine afternoon, baby. It's a weekday, you have a rare day off from school, the predicted snow never came and the temps are holding steady. We decide to first visit the brand-new Little Library installed right on the grounds of City Hall in our little city's downtown.

But that's not enough for you. We have time. You have energy. There are snacks around every corner, and anything seems possible.

"Okay, let's do it," I say. "Where shall we explore?"

"The library!" you say.

I'm thrilled to hear that exploration to you means going to the library; such would have been my response at your age. The trouble is that we're not near the library.

"No, Daddy, we are. I remember we are."

"The library is on the other side of town, baby, too far to walk."

But you're adamant. "No, it's by the drawings of the cats, where's the cats?"

And then I put it together. It's not the library you're thinking of, it's the bookstore. And the kitty murals are in an alley next to the bookstore called Cat Alley. This all makes perfect sense.

"Got it!" I say. "Let's explore!"

Richard Campbell, the Restoration Director of the Save the Redwoods League, writes about finding wildness in the most unlikely of places. Instead of thinking about nature in cities as manicured parks and designed walking paths, he suggests focusing your attention on the "abandoned and unruly places."

"The flowers that grow through the cracks in an old foundation teach us of resilience and patience and the power of life," he writes. "The butterflies that emanate from the lot inspire delight and curiosity."

So let's do that today, baby.

"Let's find some animals," I suggest.

You give me a half glance, a look that I've come to understand means something like, "I'm with you, but I think you might be crazy."

But I know just the place. Running for a couple hundred feet next to City Hall is a mini strip of park and pathway. Enclosed by buildings yet teaming with plants and dirt, we head there, and you take right to it. You follow the red bricks like a tiny Dorothy. You pick some orange leaves off the ground and shove them into your pockets. But most exciting of all, you shriek—and I know our little walk has been successful.

You're pointing. "Look at him, Daddy, look at him!"

Sitting happily on a tree branch nearly at eye level to you is a chubby, chirping squirrel. He's looking right at you. I suspect, given our location, this may be some wildlife that's used to getting fed along this path.

Very carefully, you step up over the curb to a section of

mulched trees and shrubs, and tiptoe toward your newest gray friend. You look back at me once for confirmation that this is allowed. I nod, and the chase is on.

Remarkably, the little fellow allows you to get close, maybe four feet, before skittering to a new branch where he turns around and looks again. You follow and get to within another three or four feet before he moves again. You follow.

This follow and move goes on for a long time, like he's leading you someplace, like he's playing with you. And he's not a small squirrel, either. He hops up, turns to look back, quivers his furry tail, and you skip toward him giggling; a little human and a rodent engaged in tree ballet.

Finally, your playmate heads off to find bigger trees, and perhaps snacks. And we do as well.

At the bookstore, we settle into a corner with some blank pages and a couple tins of colored pencils. From out of nowhere, you find a group of little wooden robots and trace their outlines onto the paper.

"Now, we're going to draw them like how they look," you announce. "You do that one."

"Any color or black like they are?"

"Oh no, in color," you say. "All the colors. This one will have rainbow feet."

So there we are—dad and daughter—on a weekday, surrounded by the noise and bustle of a city, coloring robot feet. This is an often-challenging accomplishment, this art of deliberately doing nothing. The Italians have a name for it, *la dolce far niente*, or the sweetness of doing nothing.

I have no moral today, no lesson or epiphany. Sometimes,

just *being* is enough. I will say this though: There is nothing more important, right here right now, than the complicated happenstance of two humans, sipping coffee and apple juice, coloring robots—an island within an island—as the world whirls by us, and we just stay still and do nothing, and do everything.

WHAT YOU BELIEVE

Out of the blue, from the back seat of the car, you say, "Daddy, dragons aren't real."

This is a sharp stab, an ambush, a surprise attack on the very foundation of my parenting process and expectations. Devastating!

I'm not a fan of dragons, baby, though they did play a big role in my Dungeons and Dragons days.

Still, in four words you've laid bare the undeniable truth of becoming an adult—that is to say, you stop believing. A truth I attempted to curtail you from reaching—a truth which you've helped me reclaim.

Having you in my life allowed me to shuck off the leaden restraints of disbelief, to be more mindful and less cynical. Every morning I'm able to wake up and understand that awe and wonder are once again part of my life. I don't believe in dragons, perhaps, but through your eyes I've seen wondrous things I can't explain, had moments of epiphany almost daily, and I am grateful for every moment we spend together.

And now this. As one of the foremost authorities on dragons, J.R.R. Tolkien once wrote, "So comes snow after fire, and even dragons have their endings." Is this the end of your belief, baby?

At the edge of the maps and globes the ancients used to

make, there was always the head or tail of a dragon or some other beastie lurking about—a reminder that they didn't really have any idea what was out there. The phrase, "Here be dragons," a rejoinder to suggest danger of the unknown, comes out of those early globes.

So here we are, just a kid and her dad, talking about dragons that you no longer believe exist.

"What makes you say that, baby?" I ask.

"I dunno, just they're too big, I guess."

This is a crossroads of the sort that, my guess is, parents have been having to deal with for a long time. Do I argue in favor of dragons and try to convince you? Do you need assurances that dragons are, in fact, real if even symbolically? Or, do we let this one go, and redouble my efforts to reinforce the Santa/Magic firewall?

Study after study has shown the disturbing fact that kids are rejecting their belief in magic earlier and earlier, some suggesting that the magic is gone as early as six or seven years old.

Health and parenting writer Seema Iyer writes that what I'm feeling is actually fairly common, that I'm equating a drop off in fantastical belief with a loss of innocence. And I don't wish for you to lose your innocence.

"One argument for this loss of wonderment is the world being more depressing," she writes. "Children are aware that these problems are not being solved with spells and magic. And that depressing reality may also be feeding into this rejection of the fantastical."

And while I'm not so certain the world is any more or less depressing for children than it ever has been, I do agree that as you get older, you begin to understand better how the world works. And it requires some effort and self-awareness to make the jump from believing in magic to believing that science and culture and tradition can be magical.

Still, it would be nice to find a place for dragons.

"Do you think dragons ever existed?" I ask.

"No," you say. Do I detect a hint of sadness? After a long pause, you continue, "But I'm afraid of goblins!"

"Really? Goblins? What do they look like?"

"Blobby and smelly."

"Why are you afraid of them?"

"I dunno, they're scary and loud. They don't like fairies, though."

"Who?"

"Goblins."

"So fairies exist though, right?"

"Yup."

I know parents who never peddle in myths and legends, and I sort of get the reasoning—a kid can't be disappointed by Santa (or even worse, catch your parents in a multi-year elaborate lie) if there is never a Santa to begin with. But I recall a handful of years at my aunt's house where my dad swore we could actually see Santa flying by out the window if we were patient enough. I spent a lot of time looking out that window. And that one year where my uncle actually went out on the roof while I was looking and made it seem like Santa had landed. Imagine my surprise when Santa himself came down the stairs. (Actually, my aunt, who I never noticed had disappeared, played the role.) Core memories like that are priceless.

"How do you know fairies exist, baby?" I ask.

You make a clicking sound, like you're scolding me for asking a dumb question. "Because Tinker Bell is a fairy, and she helps the Tooth Fairy and she left me a note when my tooth came out."

"Right."

I wonder if a dragon phone app would be as successful as the Tooth Fairy one is, the one where you can "film" the Tooth Fairy leaving your kid's bedroom window.

The actual evidence of the existence of the magic is what drills the concept home; the cookies that disappear on Christmas Day or the reindeer food we put out on the front lawn or the note from Tinker Bell.

But you're not done. "Daddy, fairies live in a fairyland above the clouds."

"Oh yeah," I say, "I forgot."

So we've gone from dragons to goblins to fairies and the world appears to still be—somewhat—magical to you. Soon, we'll have to make the leap—from magic to imagination, from literal to symbolic—and that's fine. Smaug, King Ghidorah, and Falkor are as much a part of my DNA now as they were then—that never goes away.

But I do hope you hold on to the real for just a little bit longer, baby. Go slow. The world is better with Santa and fairies and ghosts. My world is better because you believe, and I guess I'm not ready yet to let go of dragons.

LITTLE GIRL HOWLING

On a warm Christmas Eve night, high on a hill overlooking your city, surrounded by family and friends, you are lifted up by an elder, turned toward the woods, and you howl to the wolves with all the might of your nearly five-year-old lungs.

We are celebrating Wigilia, the traditional Polish Christmas Eve vigil supper. Our close friends have invited your whole family to take part in this deeply personal tradition. As is the case with all centuries-old rites, each tradition takes on new meaning and creates and recreates itself over the years within the context of the family doing the celebrating. For weeks now, ever since we were invited, you've been practicing your wolf call.

Your critical role in this celebration is one that, sadly, I don't remember at all from my own family's celebrations. (Though when asked, your aunt—my sister—seems to remember some sort of yelling or howling going on during our Christmas Eve dinners at our aunt's home. I have no memory of that.)

This old country ritual dates back to farming times, when families were concerned over the predatory nature of wolves coming onto the grounds and attacking the chicken coops or eating stored food. On the night before Christmas, right before supper is served, the eldest family member and the youngest step outside and call to the wolves, inviting them to the table. If the wolves fail to come, then the family farm is protected for another year.

You've taken your job seriously these past few days, practicing endlessly. You are wearing wolf ears. You brought your furry friend, Howly the Wolf, to lend you strength.

Your partner is Mr. Tom, or Poppa Bear as he is affectionately called by his children and family. He is the patriarch on this evening, the carrier of tradition, the one who hosts the night. You met him a few months ago, briefly, and I had concerns that you might be too shy when the time came. But you've practiced too hard, waited too long, to turn back. You are committed.

The time will come after the Wolf Call to dig into homemade sausage and pierogi made by our hosts, and to feast on the momos made by your own mother and grandmother. There is a Yankee Swap waiting for us, and babka and kapusta and cake forged from passed-down recipes. And piles of cookies. Even later, a grand fire will rage, warming the home and our bones.

For now, though, Poppa Bear finishes with the prayers and the toasts and announces the time has come to call the wolves. You jump right to the front of the crowd and hold his hand as the two of you make your way to the sliding doors, flung open to the evening chill. And then one last surprise: Poppa Bear lifts you up, and you two—with nearly seventy years separating you, no longer strangers, the bookends to tradition and family—step into the darkness.

"Ready?" he says. "Now!"

You raise your chin to the air and howl, pure and smooth—
and for those few seconds, there is no other sound on earth.
And I think, if there are wolves out there, they'll let us be
because they now know one of their own haunts that beautiful,
bright home high on a hill on the day before Christmas.

Poppa Bear recites the mantra, in Polish, warning off the
wickedness of the wolves, assuring that by inviting the preda-
tor to the table, the family will be safe for another year.

The guests applaud the ritual, the doors are closed, and the
feast of gratitude begins in earnest. Later, I catch you staring
wistfully out the window.

"Daddy," you say, "do you think they'll come?"

"The wolves, baby? I'm guessing that they will not."

You sigh, because you are who you are, my kindhearted
child, and to you that howl was not a warning, but rather an
eager summons, a call of sisterhood.

I put my arm around you. "Well, if they do come, what
shall we offer them?" I ask.

You think for a moment. "Cake?"

"Wolves would love cake, I'm certain."

This seems to satisfy you. The home buzzes with tradition,
gifts are exchanged, and coffee is brewed. Yet another ritual is
added to the toolbox of your life, and someplace down toward
the river, your howl still echoes off the glass and the concrete
of the quiet city, and the air is alive with the breath of a little
girl's invitation.

EPILOGUE

And so, my stardust child, my organic alarm clock—where will we go from here?

You're familiar with me now. And I, you. In our connection, there is comfort; even on days when my patience is short, even on days when you misstep.

You are literally awash in possibility. And you're old enough now to begin to have some say in your journey. But I can tell you what I wish for you.

I want you to experience epiphanies that crack you open as you do to me every day—a new door of perception opening every time you learn a new word, connect your imagination to a real-world concept, or tell me you love me. Or you love a stuffed animal. Or you love a grasshopper.

I wish for you to transcend mere perception, to dig deeply into culture and morality and your own sense of your place on this blue and green rock as I have been able to, because of you.

Watching you grow and learn in everyday, mundane steps continues to feel transformative. And I'm shocked at how a simple few moments—just you swinging on a handrail or grinning as you pose atop an old alley backdoor—can feel so revelatory. When you give two peace signs, I wonder, where did you learn that?

This is the place where we all secretly (or not so secretly) desire to return, to that child-like state of awe and reverence where every pebble and every cloud fills us with wonder like a balloon full of helium lifted up by the romance of living.

You know how exciting and terrifying it feels to experience something for the first time. When is the last time an adult has done that? But for you, baby, those first experiences happen all the time, every day, over and over. You are flooded minute by minute with fresh input.

I'm haunted by this desire to keep returning to the present. Some days are a struggle because all I feel is either anxiety over the future or melancholy about the past. But you're engaged, you're able to bring me into the now. Fiercely. Time and again.

The writer Michael Pollen suggests that we are all seeking that "sense of first sight, unencumbered by knowingness." We have to unlearn the structure that we built to make sense of the world, because sometimes that structure of life becomes a prison. It's like I want to forget everything I know and learn it new every day with you.

How I wish sometimes that I could hold Play-Doh or a cotton ball for the first time. Oh, to taste a dumpling for the first time. To see a fish. To hear "Let it Be." To ride the downtown trolley with your mother for the first time again.

That first time has a hold on us. Your first times are epiphanies, tiny life-changing explosions. You give this back to me, baby. Watching your wide eyes is a window out—like being in a room and looking out the glass and wishing I was out there instead of in here. You open that window.

You are, at heart, a Romantic poet, a carrier of both the pain and joy of life—the eternal flame of the paradox of feeling. You may not know it, you may not be able to give voice to your power quite yet, but someday, I hope, you'll look back and see what you did.

You'll understand, as all the great poets have, that eternity can be found in a minute. You'll see that every time you handed me a wildflower, I entered Nirvana.

Our journey is the reason why Mary Oliver wrote,

> Everyday
> I see or hear
> something
> that more or less
> kills me
> with delight.

I see your smile and I understand what Lord Byron understood when he wrote, "The great object of life is sensation." This moment with you, whatever moment it may be, reminds me of what Whitman meant when he wrote, "Happiness, knowledge, not in another place, but this place, not for another hour, but this hour."

This morning, you collect a dozen rocks from our backyard, placing each of them delicately into a little basket that you found someplace. Not special rocks. Not painted. Not mica. No quartz. Just grey slabby rocks. I think a couple of them are actually tar. Then, as we're leaving for school, you bring the basket with you.

"Daddy, I want to give the rocks to my friends," you say.

Street rocks, covered in dirt, unimaginably dull and dispensable in every way. Rocks. But in selecting them as gifts, you have imbued the everyday with meaning. We could go our entire adult lives without even seeing the rocks beneath our toes; we give no thought to the drab. But you've been able to turn nothing into a gift.

What do you learn from these moments of transformation? How do I teach you to hold on to them? Better yet, how do I learn from them—am I able to recognize the ways in which you teach me to be a better dad?

We seek to grasp meaning, baby; we travel to find home. We look too often to the horizon for enlightenment when it's right here, all around us, every day. Like Ken Kesey getting "tuned in" and Einstein finding "liberation within the self."

Some of the greatest minds in history have grappled with this stuff, baby, and here you are at five years old, turning rocks into jewels and handing them out like candy.

Thanks for the years of enlightenment, little Buddha girl. Where do we go from here? Nowhere and everywhere. We drift on, arms and voices raised, carried ceaselessly on the stardust.

ACKNOWLEDGMENTS

There is a moment in my memory—sharp and clearly focused, just minutes after my daughter was delivered—of a nurse reaching out and taking my elbow as my wife was being wheeled to surgery.

Her name, I'd find out later, was Deb Crowly Grant.

She whispered in my ear, "She's being taken now across the way; she is in very good hands. Now would be the time to tell her you love her."

And I did. That was five years ago and, of course, everything turned out fine, eventually.

We've become friends with Deb since that day, and I'd be remiss to not begin by thanking Deb and the entire staff on call in maternity and ICU at Elliot Hospital in Manchester that worked tirelessly not just to save Meena's life and keep Uma safe, but also to keep me from losing my mind.

They protected me and walked me through the days that followed with an empathy we don't often assign to nurses and doctors. They even let me raid the ward fridge for Popsicles. We owe them a great debt.

And to all the friends, family and readers who have reached out through the years to offer hand-me-downs, advice, play dates, home-cooked meals, rides, baby-sitting, kindness, smiles, or they just—somehow—enjoyed these frequent musings about life, love, diaper changes, and everyday expressions of awe, thank you. I heard all of it, and I appreciate it more than you can imagine.

Whether you have kids or not, whether they are small, big, or not yet here—whether your pup, bunny, or kitty are your kids, we are all in some way or another in it together.

So, thank you to everyone who has hitched a ride; thank you to Chris, Nicole and Oscar Aubin, Fred and Anne-Louie Bailey, Ken Bennett, Jen Drociak, Linda Feinberg, Beth Gallaway, David Graves, Steve Laurin, Bill Millios, Aaron Mylott, Janelle Mylott, Peter, Elizabeth and Isla Noonan, Gregory Norris, Ed Pacht, Jeff Rapsis, Ron Klopfanstein, Michael Rodrigues, Marlene Rosenow, Alan Sobkowiak and Jennifer Wall, Keith Spiro, Mark Truman, Terri Miller Upstill, Jackie Verville, and many, many more who have encircled and loved us though the years.

To the generous writers who provided kind blurbs for the book, thank you to Brady Carlson, Christopher Diloreto, Kourtney Lafavre, Kasey Matthews, and Zoe Wroten-Heinzmann.

Many of these essays were tested, spoken out loud or written in various forms to writer groups or organizations along the way. Thanks to the New Hampshire Writers' Project, the *Monadnock Underground*, the Berlin Writers Group, the First Friday Coffee House and the United Methodist Church of Lowell in New York for the platform and community.

Big gratitude to the amazing members of the Butt-Kickin' Nano Group 2019 for supporting my yearly November writing surge.

To my family who continues to just shake their head and smile as a new project emerges around every turn. Thanks, Andrea, John, Max, Ben, Kiran, Rita, Sandeep, and Candace. Thanks, Mom. Thanks, Dad.

To my editor Susan Kennedy who gamely braves my word jungle again and again and somehow manages to make it all better.

To the good folks at Hobblebush Books—to Sid Hall for giving me a shot, and to my publisher Kirsty Walker for the advice, layout, design, and for mainly just letting me do my thing.

Finally, to the bravest and strongest human I know, and somehow, she's my wife. Thank you, Meenakshi, for being her mom; just hearing the two of you laugh together is an epiphany every time.

And after all this time, still, to Baby U—you burn like a super nova and the universe bends toward you. I can only hope to be worthy of your fire.

ABOUT THE AUTHOR

Dan Szczesny is a longtime journalist, author and speaker living in New Hampshire.

He's written several books of travel memoir (*The Adventures of Buffalo and Tough Cookie, Mosquito Rain*), fiction (*Sing and Other Stories*) and poetry (*Invincible One, Poems*).

His book, *The Nepal Chronicles*, about a month long trek to Everest Base Camp and marriage in Kathmandu, won the 2016 New Hampshire State Library award for Outstanding Work of Non-Fiction.

His most recent book, *The White Mountain: Rediscovering Mount Washington's Hidden Culture* won the 2019 New Hampshire Writer's Project award for Outstanding Work of Non-Fiction, and won the People's Choice Award for Non-Fiction that year as well.

Dan is also the Editor of Murder Ink, a series of New England-based pulp fiction anthologies set in or around the newsroom.

His short story, "White Like Marble," was a finalist in the 2017 Ernest Hemingway Foundation Short Shorts Contest, out of the Hemingway Birthplace in Oak Park, Illinois.

Dan began his career in Buffalo, New York. Since then, he has written for a wide variety of regional and national publications, including the *Main Line Times, Philadelphia Weekly,*

Christian Science Monitor, Princeton Packet, Pennsylvania Magazine, Appalachia Journal, New Hampshire Magazine, AMC Outdoors, Yahoo! Parenting and *Huffington Post*.

In 2000, he moved to New Hampshire to cover the presidential election. In 2001, Dan became associate publisher of *The Hippo*, now the state's largest arts and entertainment journal.

He's a member of the Appalachian Mountain Club's 4,000-footer club and has written extensively about the outdoors and hiking. He has camped in the Grand Canyon, hiked England's Coast-to-Coast, trail and trekked to Everest Base Camp in Nepal. Dan was a hiking guide and naturalist for Blue Hill Observatory and Science Center in Milton, Massachusetts.

Dan lives in Manchester with his wife and Baby U. For more on Dan's books, visit www.danszczesny.com.

ALSO BY DAN SZCZESNY

The White Mountain
(Hobblebush Books, 2018)

Invincible One, Poems
(EKP Books, 2017)

Mosquito Rain, Alaskan Travel Essays
(Folded Word, 2016)

Sing, and Other Short Stories
(Hobblebush Books, 2015)

*The Nepal Chronicles: Marriage, Mountains
and Momos in the Highest Place on Earth*
(Hobblebush Books, 2014)

The Adventures of Buffalo and Tough Cookie
(Bondcliff Books, 2013)

THE HOBBLEBUSH REFLECTIONS SERIES

The Hobblebush Reflections Series provides an avenue for sharing in-depth observations about our most important moments and the minutiae of everyday life. Each volume is written by one author and consists of short essays or musings on a specific topic. For more information, visit www.hobblebush.com.